To Joshua,
With b...

Do you love reading literatu
novels and stories of the Vi........ .... Edwardian eras?
Are you someone who may have read them when you were
younger and forgotten their delights and delectations?
Could you be one of those many souls that passed the aisles
of classic novels in a thousand book shops, but simply
never got around to picking one up? Or perhaps you even
thought they might be boring?

Whether you have discovered classic novels or not, acclaimed author and international book illustrator **Jonathan Barry** has written this book for you. It is his attempt to encourage you to read and explore a personal selection of what he regards as twelve of the greatest classic stories ever written in the English language, and to explain *WHY* you should read them.

Jonathan is a lifelong passionate exponent of these famous tales and has illustrated all twelve of them in his career as a professional book illustrator (he has illustrated over seventy famous classic titles). In this careful selection of twelve of his favourite stories (supported by his artwork) he offers a very personal view of why everybody who loves reading should delve into these great works of fiction from a golden age of literature. He believes that to read them is a deeply rewarding experience that will give a lifetime of pleasure. Enjoy.

Oct 25, 2024

— On your Graduation — -

Love,

Paul & Elene

GREAT CLASSIC STORIES
(From the Victorian and Edwardian eras)

And Why You Should Read Them.

A Personal View

Written and illustrated

By
JONATHAN BARRY

Glass Darkly Press
Dublin
2024

Published in 2024 by
Glass Darkly Press, Dublin, Ireland.

Text Copyright Jonathan Barry, 2024
Front cover design and typeset: Kervin Arias.
All illustrations and artwork Copyright Jonathan Barry, 2024

ISBN: 978-1-3999-6882-9

First Edition.

Set in Crimson Pro 13 on 15.6 pt.
Printed in Ireland.

I once again dedicate this book to three people.

Firstly, to my late lovely father, **John Barry** (1929 – 2015) himself a skilled pianist, organist, trombonist, and boy soprano, who gave me a lifetime's passion for music, literature, novels, and the movies. He taught me the values of kindness, compassion, dignity, and courage.

Secondly, to my beloved late friend, **Brother Declan Murphy** (1930 – 2016), of Mount Mellery Abbey, in Waterford, Ireland, for over forty years of unfailing friendship, consummate wisdom, memorable walks together, joy and laughter, and human understanding.

Finally, to my mother, **Maureen Barry** (who discovered I could draw, write, and paint), I owe a lifetime of gratitude for her endless creative input, tireless encouragement, and unflinching support.

CONTENTS

INTRODUCTION

The purpose of this book is to encourage adults and children alike to read and discover a careful selection of twelve of the greatest classic stories ever written in the English language. All of these famous tales are from the golden age of the Victorian and Edwardian eras, which marked one of the watersheds in the history of literary creativity and quality writing. From 1837 to 1910 there was an explosion of some of the most original, memorable, powerful, and ground-breaking novels and children's stories, ever put to paper.

It should be made clear that this is not an academic work, although I myself have quite literally dedicated my entire life to books: whether it is reading them, writing them, illustrating them, painting oil paintings based on them, discussing them at my book club, giving talks and lectures on them, collecting them, celebrating them, or watching movies based on them. Ever since I could walk and talk – books have enthralled and enraptured me. A life without books is for me a definition of hell – a torturous and barren journey worthy of Dante's *Inferno*. It is my hope to pass on in this modest offering some of my genuine love and enthusiasm for several of my favourite novels and stories, by explaining *why* they are worthy of exploration and remembrance.

Where did I get this passion from? One explanation is that I must consider myself very fortunate to have grown up in a house and home teeming from floor to ceiling with books – tomes of every distinction and genre, piled high on my father's multitudinous antique bookcases (most of which were Edwardian themselves, made of blackened aged oak, with sliding glass doors, which my father had bought in London). The smell alone of these mysterious charming bookcases made me want to open them as a boy – never mind what was in them.

But oh, when my father took one of them out of the bookcase (when I was thirteen years of age), and then gave it to me as a gift, to start me on my lifelong literary adventures – that was a fabulous moment indeed. The book he happened to give me was a burgundy-coloured leatherette antiquarian edition of Charles Dickens' *A Christmas Carol*. The scent of the binding, the sparkle of the gold gilded page edges, made me fall in love with it immediately. But when I also read it from cover to cover and realised what a marvellous story it was – then I became consumed with wanting more, and I never looked back. Through my teenage years I became enamoured with the classics, and threw myself headlong into the worlds of the Brontës, Dickens, Poe, H. G. Wells, Robert Louis Stevenson, Arthur Conan Doyle, Oscar Wilde, H. Rider Haggard, Bram Stoker, and a host of other great writers. I was like the proverbial child – only this time in a literary sweetshop.

As well as discovering the talents of these formidable authors – I was also introduced to some of the world's greatest book illustrators whose artwork adorned many of these famous volumes. The fantastic drawings and watercolours of Arthur Rackham, Edmund Dulac, Phiz (H.K. Browne), E. H. Shepherd, Kay Nielsen, Sidney Paget, John Tenniel, all became inspirational to me. So much so, that by the time I reached my eighteenth birthday I already knew that I wanted to become a book illustrator and author. Through mainly hard work, late nights, some application, and a modicum of luck – I managed to do just that.

But I stress that it was the inspiration and love of the twelve classic stories, that I discuss here in this book, that helped spur me on to want to make it as a writer and illustrator. They formed a vital backdrop to my own imagination, and repeated readings of these masterly works have sustained and lifted me when creativity has not always answered my call. I have also been fortunate to have had the chance to illustrate all twelve of these tales in my career as a book illustrator.

And that is what I wish to share with you, dear reader - my heartfelt love of these timeless works. I believe that every human being should know these stories, as they will open up a glorious vein of pleasure, joy, inspiration, insight, and understanding, both of ourselves, and the world around us. Here is your excuse to now take that first step.

Jonathan Barry, 2024.

I

Wuthering Heights
By
Emily Brontë
(1818 – 1848)

Wuthering Heights is one of the greatest novels ever written, and anyone with a passion for literature must read this extraordinary work. Cast aside any pre-conceived notions that you may have garnered from botched movie attempts or TV adaptations. The original novel remains as powerful, beautiful, and disturbing today, as when it first revealed itself to an unsuspecting public in 1847. *Wuthering Heights* is not just an exceptional novel - it is a Gothic masterpiece of artistic vision, spun together by the literary genius of Emily Brontë's imagination. It surprised readers then, and it still dazzles and lures us today.

So what marks it out as a must read? There are several compelling reasons to enter its dark world: there is Emily Brontë's superb fluid modern prose, her delicious turn of phrase, the novel's unique setting and atmosphere, the outstanding romantic protagonists that are Cathy and Heathcliff, its striking supernatural undercurrents, and its memorable scenes that can never be forgotten by the reader.

Great prose writers are not as common as you think, but Emily was one of the finest. It's hard to believe that someone so young could write with such maturity as a first time novelist. She was only 19 when she started writing it, and most Brontë scholars believe that she completed the text by her 24th birthday - a fine achievement in itself. But what stands out to anyone reading *Wuthering Heights* today is the absolute modernity of the prose. It reads like a novel that could have been written in the 21st century. Her style is fluid, clear, confident, and eminently readable to all age groups. At times it resembles a movie screenplay, and sadly, it was to be her only novel.

Her descriptive skills are a major strength in her narrative, especially with geographical landscapes. Look how she describes the brutal natural setting of the building Wuthering Heights:

> ...one may guess the power of the north wind, blowing over the edge, by the excessive slant of a few, stunted firs at the end of the house; and by a range of gaunt thorns all stretching their limbs one way, as if craving alms of the sun.[1]

It is that beautiful little phrase "craving alms of the sun" which is so typical of Emily's poetic powers. In the hands of a lesser writer these ordinary thorn bushes might have been described in a dull fashion. But not Emily. To her it is a chance to imbue a plain shrub with an almost spiritual living quality.

Which brings us nicely to the story's unique setting on the blasted heaths of the Yorkshire moors. It was the first time

"Cathy and Heathcliff"

Oil on canvas, 2009.

Copyright © artist Jonathan Barry.

a major romantic novel was located on this wild landscape. Emily, along with her siblings Charlotte, Anne, Branwell, and their father Patrick, lived in the quiet village of Haworth, West Yorkshire, in a modest house called The Parsonage. Every day she walked the same ten or twelve miles over the moors which she adored, and it was there that she gleaned all of the locations for her tempestuous tale.

When I myself was asked to illustrate *Wuthering Heights* some years ago - I visited the Brontë Parsonage on several occasions. To research my drawings I walked all of the moors that Emily tread each day, and visited the same ruins, buildings, and natural landmarks that she was familiar with.

I was struck by the astonishing beauty of the Haworth moors and felt as if I was transposed into the living breathing world of the novel. My visits to the ruin called 'Top Withens' (which Emily used as her model for the fictional building of Wuthering Heights) left me mightily impressed with its close resemblance to the doomed house in the story. Emily had a brilliant eye for choosing a dramatic architectural structure.

Similarly, when I hiked a further mile and a half over the moors from 'Top Withens' I stumbled across 'Ponden Hall' a beautiful and still occupied Tudor home from the late 1580s (extended and rebuilt by Robert Heaton in 1634), which Emily used as her model for Thrushcross Grange. As I stood admiring the venerable coursed stone of this structure I noticed the latticed ground floor living room window, which reminded me strongly of Heathcliff's description of the window he and Cathy look into in Chapter 6, when they visit Thrushcross Grange in the dark. I felt as if I were close to them somehow, even though they are only fictional creations. Heathcliff describes what he sees to Nelly Dean when he says:

> We crept through a broken hedge, groped our way up the path, and planted ourselves on a flower-pot under the drawing-room window. The light came from thence; they had not put up the shutters, and the curtains were only half closed. Both of us were able to look in by standing on the basement, and clinging to the ledge, and we saw – ah! it was beautiful – a splendid place carpeted with crimson, and crimson-covered chairs and tables, and a pure white ceiling bordered by gold, a shower of glass-drops hanging in silver chains from the centre, and shimmering with little soft tapers.

And further up the moors I climbed to the top of 'Penistone Crag' (better known in the local area as Ponden Kirk), a real life stone promontory that Emily adapted as the romantic meeting place for Cathy and Heathcliff whenever they wished to be alone. I was in awe of the natural beauty of each of these places.

It is impossible to stand there and not imagine the two doomed lovers arm in arm, especially in Emily's evocative description of their ramblings:

"Penistone Crag"

Oil on canvas, 1996.

Copyright © artist Jonathan Barry.

But it was one of their chief amusements to run away to the moors in the morning, and remain there all day, and the after punishment grew a mere thing to laugh at.

Having established this perfect natural stage - she then develops the two most passionate romantic characters of all time - Cathy and Heathcliff. Their creation is a testament to her powerful imagination because we know that Emily was a recluse who never had a romantic relationship with anyone.

Heathcliff is a remarkable invention - a dark, handsome, brooding, possessive, violent and mercurial brute, who exudes a form of animal magnetism and masculinity that female readers cannot resist. If he was a real person living in the 21st century he might be regarded as a thug, a sexual predator, and could possibly even be jailed as a violent partner. But this is Emily's most extraordinary achievement - despite the fact that we the reader are horrified by Heathcliff's violent excesses - we still feel for his predicament and identify with his hurt and pain. Deep down we believe that he has been cheated in life and that his love for Cathy is pure and justified. He is a tragic victim with whom we can identify and sympathize.

Cathy is no less alluring: beautiful, intelligent, wild, coquettish, obstinate, sensitive and beguiling. In Chapter 9, in one of the most famous scenes in the book she pours out her heart to Nelly Dean the housekeeper, describing her feelings for Heathcliff when she says:

My love for Heathcliff resembles the eternal rocks beneath: a source of little visible delight, but necessary. Nelly, I am Heathcliff! He's always, always in my mind: not as a pleasure, any more than I am always a pleasure to myself, but as my own being.

And this really is the fulcrum around which the entire novel rotates. Cathy and Heathcliff are the two halves of one soul and until they are united they will languish in misery. Tragically of course they both die alone and separated. But Emily does strongly imply in the final chapter that they do find peace as their souls unite in their final resting place together.

It is this implied hint of a supernatural sub-text throughout the story which has made *Wuthering Heights* a recognized Gothic masterpiece. The appearance of the child spectre of Cathy during the snowstorm of Chapter 3, is one of the most moving and haunting ghost scenes in the history of literature. Lockwood (Heathcliff's tenant) is awoken by what he thinks is a tiny branch rubbing against his window. Unable to unlock the hasp he grows frustrated and we read:

> I rose and endeavoured to unhasp the casement. The hook was soldered into the staple, a circumstance observed by me, when awake, but forgotten. 'I must stop it nevertheless!' I muttered, knocking my knuckles through the glass, and stretching an arm out to seize the importunate branch: instead of which, my fingers closed on the fingers of a little, ice-cold hand!

"Heathcliff Returns"

Oil on canvas, 1993.

Copyright © artist Jonathan Barry.

Anyone who has read this passage for the first time can never forget it, and I remember getting goose bumps and chills as a fourteen year old devouring this vignette of terror. It is the first in a series of similarly striking episodes in the novel which demonstrates the intense feelings that bind Cathy and Heathcliff together. If there is one word that defines their relationship - it is 'passion'.

This dangerous 'passion' that each holds for the other becomes increasingly desperate and violent, culminating in Cathy's untimely and unnecessary death. In what is regarded as one of the highlights of 19th century drama – the recounting of Heathcliff's anguish in Chapter 16, as he learns of Cathy's passing away – is powerful indeed. All of us who have lost loved ones on this earth feel for his agony. Nelly Dean describes his hysterical outbursts:

'Be with me always – take any form – drive me mad! only do not leave me in this abyss, where I cannot find you! Oh God! it is unutterable! I cannot live without my life! I cannot live without my soul!'

He dashed his head against the knotted trunk; and, lifting up his eyes, howled, not like a man, but like a savage beast getting goaded to death with knives and spears. I observed several splashes of blood about the bark of the tree, and his hand and forehead were both stained; probably the scene I witnessed was a repetition of others acted during the night.

Wuthering Heights has one of the best closing sentences ever penned in a novel. It displays once again Emily Brontë's poetic prowess. Nelly Dean who is standing over Heathcliff and Cathy's graves says:

> I lingered around them, under that benign sky; watched the moths fluttering among the heath and harebells; listened to the soft wind breathing through the grass; and wondered how anyone could ever imagine unquiet slumbers, for the sleepers in that quiet earth.

When you have completed reading the book I would thoroughly recommend following it up with a viewing of the excellent three part BBC TV adaptation from 1978, starring Ken Hutchison as Heathcliff, Kay Adshead as Cathy, and John Duttine as a complex Hindley. This was the only version that kept faithfully to the structure, dialogue, and intensity of the book.

II

The Wind in the Willows
By
Kenneth Grahame
(1859 – 1932)

If you wish to go to bed with a broad smile on your face and a warm glow in your heart then read *The Wind in the Willows*. It is a joyous evocation of everything that is wonderful in life. There are only a handful of great children's fantasy stories that appeal so equally to either a child reader or an appreciative adult. But this book achieves exactly that with grace and charm, which is why it has been adored by generations of adults and children since it was first published in 1908. The word 'beautiful' can often be overused as a jaded adjective, but in this case it is completely justified.

The Wind in the Willows is a truly beautiful tale which celebrates and draws attention to the full glory of the British countryside, including England's rivers, mills, fields, woods, animals, flora and fauna. And it deliberately uses this backdrop to capture a nostalgic snapshot (albeit a fictional one) of Edwardian England at the height of its optimism, before the arrival of the horrors of World War I.

Central to its themes are the importance of friendship, loyalty, decency, affection, and the joy of living. This is remarkable in itself when we consider that Kenneth Grahame suffered a good deal of sadness and tragedy in his own life, with his mother dying young and his father becoming an alcoholic. He originally wrote the story to read to his only son and child Alastair, who was born blind in one eye and plagued all his life with ill health. Each night his father would read him several written pages of the text to try to bring him comfort and hope (sadly Alastair later committed suicide when he was twenty years old). It is precisely these painful memories which may explain why Grahame was so determined to write an idealised story of joy and happiness. And thank God for us he did - because it works a treat.

Kenneth Grahame grew up in Berkshire and had a lifelong passion for nature, wildlife and the great outdoors. It was his uncle who introduced him to boating, fishing and picnicking along the Thames, all of which he showcases in the narrative. I myself came quite late to *The Wind in the Willows* not reading it until I was an adult. But better late than never - because I doubt I have read a story that has made me laugh, cry, and uplifted my spirits in equal measure.

It concerns four animals called Ratty, Mole, Toad and Badger who all live on or close to a fictional quintessentially English river, complete with reeds, dragonflies, moorhens, ducks and willow trees. They are the best of friends and look out for each other through good times and bad. They are talking animals and dress and behave just like humans (Grahame it seems wished to portray them as an allegory of the best of British rural society) and they inhabit a world that is safe, cosy, and steeped in tradition.

"Messing Around In Boats"

Oil on canvas, 2010.

Copyright © artist Jonathan Barry.

I remember being struck at how sophisticated and meticulously written the book was on my first reading, and eight readings later I remain in awe of Grahame's superb prose. The structure and cadence of his sentences are delicious, and any aspiring writer would do well to study his methods. Take for example the opening chapter, where Mole has been busy doing his spring-cleaning but decides to get some fresh air by going up above ground. There follows one of the most glorious depictions of a Spring day:

> The sunshine struck hot on his fur, soft breezes caressed his heated brow, and after the seclusion of the cellarage he had lived in so long the carol of happy birds fell on his dulled hearing almost like a shout. Jumping off all his four legs at once, in the joy of living and the delight of spring without its cleaning, he pursued his way across the meadow till he reached the hedge on the further side.[1]

And just moments later Mole stumbles across a river and because he has never seen one before, his excitement is overpowering. We read:

> Never in his life had he seen a river before - this sleek, sinuous, full-bodied animal, chasing and chuckling, gripping things with a gurgle and leaving them with a laugh, to fling itself on fresh playmates that shook themselves free, and were caught and held again. All was a-shake and a-shiver - glints and gleams and sparkles, rustle and swirl, chatter and bubble. The Mole was bewitched, entranced, fascinated.

Of the four main characters in the story undoubtedly the funniest is Toad. While Ratty, Mole, and Badger are all hard-working modest sensible fellows, Toad is a vain-glorious, boastful, and attention seeking creature, and his adventures take up half the book. He is a millionaire and lives in his ancestral residence called Toad Hall. Because of his great wealth he has a weakness for buying fast motorcars. This penchant for speeding lands him in hot trouble when he crashes a car that he has stolen in a moment of mad impulse. He ends up in jail. Eventually he escapes his prison cell by disguising himself dressed as a common washerwoman.

It is these scenes where Toad flees across the countryside to escape his captors that provide us with the most comic moments. He no sooner has fled the jail in Chapter 10, when he crashes a car a second time, and finds the police hot on his heels again. Racing across a field still wearing his dress, shawl and bonnet, we are given a hilarious description of the pursuit:

> About two fields off, a chauffeur in his leather gaiters and two large rural policemen were visible, running towards him as hard as they could go! Poor Toad sprang to his feet and pelted away again, his heart in his mouth. 'Oh my!' He gasped, as he panted along, 'what an ass I am! What a conceited and heedless ass!' He glanced back, and saw to his dismay that they were gaining on him. He did his best, but he was a fat animal, and his legs were short, and still they gained.

These chase sequences with Toad are often given credit by film critics as inspiring the slapstick comedy movies called 'The Keystone Cops' produced by Max Sennett from

"Poop! Poop!"

Oil on canvas, 1998.

Copyright © artist Jonathan Barry.

1912 - 1917, as it is known that Sennett was a big fan of *The Wind in the Willows.*

I have focused above on the fun and frolics of the story, but the book does have its darker and more philosophical sides too. The rock band Pink Floyd named their debut studio album after the chapter called 'The Piper at the Gates of Dawn'. This is a more enigmatic part of the tale where Ratty and Mole are out in their boat at the crack of dawn searching for little Portly, (a baby otter who has been missing for several days). Turning a bend in the river they moor their boat to a small island, and raising their heads they proceed to have a mystical experience. They find themselves in the presence of the nature God Pan, who has Portly sleeping soundly at his feet, having protected him from exposure or harm.

For many readers this scene is the highlight of the entire book, and it is easy to see why. It is succinctly written, with pathos and a delicacy of emotion. Grahame describes the moment just before they look up at Pan's face:

> Then suddenly the Mole felt a great Awe fall upon him, an awe that turned his muscles to water, bowed his head, and rooted his feet to the ground. It was no panic terror - indeed he felt wonderfully at peace and happy - but it was an awe that smote and held him and, without seeing, he knew it could only mean that some august Presence was very, very near. And still there was utter silence in the populous bird-haunted branches around them; and still the light grew and grew.

Much can be read into the significance of this scene, and I have no doubt that Kenneth Grahame was in some way portraying himself as a protective Pan, and that Portly was a representation of his own vulnerable son Alastair.

When I came to illustrate *The Wind in the Willows*, it was important to me to pay homage to the legendary E.H. Shepherd's illustrations from the famous 1931 edition. It is his artwork more than any other illustrator that is most associated with the story. His black and white pen and ink drawings perfectly capture the essence of the four main characters, and in a later edition published in 1969 Shepherd added several gorgeous new watercolour plates.

He was and remains one of greatest children's book illustrators of all time. His seminal work for *The Wind in the Willows* adds at least forty per cent extra impact to the pleasure that is gleaned by all readers of this classic, just as his famous line drawings for *Winnie The Pooh* also became inseparable from those stories. That is the finest honour that can ever be bestowed on any book illustrator both during and after their lifetime.

When you return the book to your bookshelf, I heartily recommend that you follow it up with a viewing of the delightful 1983 animated cartoon movie made by Cosgrove Hall in Manchester. This used the excellent voice talents of David Jason as Toad, and Sir Michael Hordern as Badger.

"The Piper At The Gates Of Dawn"

Oil on canvas, 1997.

Copyright © artist Jonathan Barry.

III

The War of the Worlds
By
H.G. Wells
(1866 – 1946)

The world's obsessive fascination with the Red Planet has been around for a long time, and even this century in 2021 NASA successfully landed its latest space probe named 'Perseverance' on the surface of Mars. Also, with Elon Musk's (one of the world's richest men) Space X project now regularly testing starships to send the first manned mission to Mars – suddenly science fiction has now become science fact – and all in less than a hundred years. Much of this (not all of it admittedly) can be credited to the brilliant pioneering writing of one British author, Herbert George Wells, who along with Jules Verne was one of the fathers of the science fiction novel, and certainly the most influential.

It was his ground-breaking work *The War of the Worlds,* first published in 1898, which paved the way for Martian mania. Why? Because it was the first novel in the world to contain a plot where aliens from another planet – Mars – invade and attempt to colonise the Earth, and where inter-galactic space travel was envisioned between two planets. Every single science fiction writer or movie director since its publication owes it respect and a debt of gratitude.

Wells had a long and extraordinary life – another giant of the Edwardian age. He wrote over one hundred books, was nominated for the Nobel Prize in literature four times, was one of the inventors of the science fiction genre, became a prodigious journalist and contributed hundreds of articles and short stories to the Pall Mall Gazette. He was an active socialist, a historian, a satirist, a biographer, a futurist, and a teacher. He held a Bachelor of Science Degree in Zoology, and he co-founded the charity The Diabetic Association. Not much of a slacker by any standard!

All of the above achievements would have marked Wells out as a brilliant man – but why should you read *The War of the Worlds* I hear you ask? Because it is a cracking story, that has lost none of its verve, tension, or visceral realism, and it remains a powerful warning against the catastrophic destruction of world war – between any species. The invasion of the Ukraine in February 2022 by the murderous aggression of Vladimir Putin's Russia is yet another example of the vicious horror of modern warfare, which is ever just around the corner. Wells knew this, and foretold it.

His novel is divided into two parts: Book I – The Coming Of The Martians, and, Book II – The Earth Under The Martians. In the opening page of the first chapter Wells sets the mood starkly with a portent of direst doom. An unnamed narrator who lives near Woking in Surrey in England tells us:

No one would have believed in the last years of the nineteenth century that this world was being watched keenly and closely by intelligences greater than man's and yet as mortal as his own; that as men busied themselves about their various concerns they were scrutinised and studied, perhaps almost as narrowly as a man with a microscope might scrutinise the transient creatures that swarm and multiply in a drop of water....Yet across the gulf of space, minds that are to our minds as ours are to those of the beasts that perish, intellects vast and cool and unsympathetic, regarded this earth with envious eyes, and slowly and surely drew their plans against us.[1]

Throughout the entire text Wells cleverly uses a factual on-the-spot journalistic style to narrate the story. Indeed the same unnamed narrator very closely resembles a tabloid journalist taking copious notes, and this works well, because it gives a sense of immediacy to the tale. The reader feels they are actually experiencing everything as it unfolds. Although we are told nothing specific about the profession or personal life of the narrator, he is clearly an educated, middle class, brave, conscientious, kind, and sensitive Englishman.

In August 1894 he is invited by his astronomer friend Ogilvy to go over to his observatory in Ottershaw to observe through his telescope a series of enormous flares or fireballs shooting out of the atmosphere of Mars. Both men are puzzled by this planetary activity – putting it down to volcanic eruptions spewing out from Mars' crust. These flashes of gas continue for ten nights and then stop. A few weeks later a shooting star lands at night on Horsell Common in Surrey, attracting little interest from the local population who assume it to be a meteorite. However, a suspicious Ogilvy gets up at the crack of dawn and locates the projectile buried deep in the sand pits of the Common. To his alarm he identifies that it is not a meteorite – but a metal cylinder of intelligent design – a Martian spacecraft.

There are two things I found to be wonderful in these early chapters: firstly how Wells creates a marvellous calm before the unleashing of the aliens' fury. There is little or no hint at the carnage to come, especially as the apathetic local farmers and labourers gather around the pit to idly examine the buried spaceship. Secondly, the speed at which everything we hold dear in this life and world – and how it can be suddenly wiped out – is superbly rendered in these chapters. From bitter experience of the Covid 19 pandemic in 2020/21 we have learnt of the extreme vulnerability of human life and existence – something Wells foresaw over a hundred years ago in this work.

My skin still tingles and the hairs stand up on the back of my neck each time I read the marvellous description of the first Martian creature to emerge from the unscrewed cyclinder in the fourth chapter. Try and understand the powerful effect this had on an unsuspecting reader in 1898. We read:

> I think everyone expected to see a man emerge – possibly something a little unlike us terrestrial men, but in all essentials a man. I know I did... A big greyish rounded bulk, the size, perhaps, of a bear, was rising slowly and painfully out of the cylinder. As it bulged up and caught the light, it glistened like wet leather. Two large dark-coloured eyes were

"The War Of The Worlds"

Oil on canvas, 2011.

Copyright © artist Jonathan Barry.

regarding me steadfastly The mass that framed them, the head of the thing, it was rounded, and had, one might say, a face. There was a mouth under the eyes, the lipless brim of which quivered and panted, and dropped saliva. The whole creature heaved and pulsated convulsively. A lank tentacular appendage gripped the edge of the cylinder, another swayed in the air.

We then discover in the next few chapters that the Martians have landed their cylinders all over the world and have developed sophisticated war machines with one purpose – to annihilate the human race. These are giant metallic tripods, over one hundred feet high with rotating metal heads capable of discharging two deadly weapons – either a heat ray that incinerates everything in its path, or tubes that discharge a black chemical gas that kills all who inhale it (Wells was the first writer to introduce chemical warfare into a novel). This in no way should be taken as a spoiler to the first time reader – quite the opposite. My purpose here is to point out the brilliance of his skill as a writer in depicting the immediacy, fury, and spine-chilling horror of hand to hand combat. This is one of the main reasons to read the book – Wells puts *us* at the centre of the action – we become participants in a life and death struggle. He has us on the edge of our seats during these bloodbaths, and he keeps us there.

For me the highlight of these battle scenes comes in the seventeenth chapter, where three Martian tripods advance close to the estuary of the River Thames, as they threaten to advance on London, and are intercepted by the British torpedo-ram warship called 'Thunder Child' (in the 1890s the earliest battleships were called 'dreadnoughts' – these were enormous ironclad warships carrying four heavy guns of 12 inch calibre, and carrying between six to eighteen medium range cannons of 7.5 inch calibre). It is an exhilarating action sequence, in which the 'Thunder Child' strikes a blow for humanity by blowing up and taking down two of the three Martian war machines in sequence.

Wells describes it vividly:

A flicker of flame went up through the rising steam, and then the Martian reeled and staggered. In another moment he was cut down, and a great body of water and steam shot high in the air. The guns of the Thunder Child sounded through the reek....At the sight of the Martian's collapse the captain on the bridge yelled inarticulately, and all the crowding passengers on the steamer's stern shouted together. And then they yelled again. For, surging out beyond the white tumult drove something long and black, the flames streaming from its middle parts, its ventilators and funnels spouting fire. She was still alive; the steering-gear, it seems, was intact and her engines working. She headed straight for a second Martian, and was within a hundred yards of him when the Heat-Ray came to bear. Then with a violent thud, a blinding flash, her decks, her funnels, leaped upward. The Martian staggered with the violence of her explosion, and in another moment the flaming wreckage, still driving forward with the impetus of its pace, had struck him and crumpled him up like a thing of card-board.

It would be unfair of me to say *who* wins this battle of two worlds, nor will I disclose *how* the victory comes – as that is one of the interesting twists for the first time explorer of this novel. But what stands out for me in the Epilogue is one particular quote made by the narrator at the conclusion of the war. In our own century's dark days of the Covid 19 pandemic which gripped the world from 2020 - 2021, it is difficult to read this sentence from a book published in 1898, and not feel its chilling relevance to our world today. And it was clearly Wells own belief, when, speaking through the narrator, he says:

> We have learned now that we cannot regard this planet as being fenced in and a secure abiding-place for Man; we can never anticipate the unseen good or evil that may come upon us suddenly.

Never a truer word was spoken.

When you have put the book aside, there are two adaptations worthy of note. The first was an infamous and brilliantly audacious radio production made by Orson Welles in 1938. It was broadcast live on CBS Radio in the United States, and because it began without an announcement that it was 'fiction', it caused widespread panic among many hundreds of thousands of Americans who took to the motorways, fleeing what they thought was a real Martian invasion. Despite the mayhem it caused, it was a marvellous production, and is well worth listening to.

Likewise, the 1953 movie called 'The War of the Worlds' (while being admittedly heavily Americanised) captures very well the sense of sheer panic and outright terror that the Martian onslaught creates. The frailty of human life and how quickly the simple pleasures of settled civilisation can be destroyed – are laid bare in this sharp production. It is gloriously shot in Technicolour and stars Gene Barry and Ann Robinson.

IV

The Hound of the Baskervilles
By
Arthur Conan Doyle
(1859 – 1930)

Arthur Conan Doyle was born to write, becoming one of the greatest storytellers of his generation. Words, plots and characters poured from his pen like a divine gift. No matter what the subject matter was he would present it in his own inimitable effortless style, the main hallmark of which was his eminently readable text. It was once remarked by a 20th century critic that if Conan Doyle had been asked to write a phone directory it would have been the most exquisitely written in the world - and I know exactly what he meant.

Of the sixty Sherlock Holmes stories that he wrote, undoubtedly the most famous is *The Hound of the Baskervilles*. It is one part a Gothic horror story, and one part a detective thriller mystery. It boasts a clever plot, an unforgettable haunted setting on the marshes of Dartmoor, an atmosphere of intense terror, superb dialogue, and the greatest sleuth of them all - Mr. Sherlock Holmes - at his scintillating best. When he was preparing to write the novel Conan Doyle was determined to locate it in a landscape that was dark, wild, and filled with superstition. To this end he visited and spent considerable time researching in Dartmoor in Devon. It was here that he found the perfect location for his yarn complete with local legends steeped in folklore.

For example, it was Conan Doyle's friend Bertram Fletcher Robinson who introduced him to the legend of Squire Richard Cabell (a real person), who lived at Brook Hall (a real residence), in the parish of Buckfastleigh (a real town) in Devon. Cabell was a delinquent aristocrat with a dire reputation for drinking, hunting, whoredom and violence. It was even rumoured that he murdered his own wife. When he died in 1677, local wagging tongues said that he had sold his soul to the Devil, and legend expounds that on the night of his burial a band of unruly monstrous hounds came across the moors howling and baying outside his tomb. From that day forward Cabell's spectre was said to be seen and heard roaming the moors with his hounds, on the anniversary of his death.

Conan Doyle thought this was a fitting fable, and he adapted and used it readily for his own fictional legend of Sir Hugo Baskerville (which forms the basis of the supernatural plot in his novel). In Chapter 2, when Dr. Mortimer visits Holmes at his Baker Street rooms, he unveils an old manuscript which outlines in colourful detail the Curse of the Baskervilles, brought about by the dastardly deeds of Sir Hugo. The only difference between the real Cabell legend and the fictional one in the book, is that instead of using a whole *pack* of ghostly hounds - Conan Doyle chose a *single* "enormous coal-black hound" for his monster.

"Holmes Gets A Case"

Oil on canvas, 2010.

Copyright © artist Jonathan Barry.

Having settled on this phantom beast he then turned his attention to finding a suitable Manor or Hall that would provide inspiration for his own invented Baskerville Hall. Once again Conan Doyle's excellent research in Devon turned up the perfect location - this time the gloomy ruins of Fowelscombe Manor (which still exist today) in the parish of Ugborough. When I was preparing my own research for illustrating *The Hound of the Baskervilles* I went to the trouble of visiting Fowelscombe Manor myself (I was living and working in London at the time) to see if indeed there was a resemblance between this building and what is described in the book.

In Chapter 6, for instance, while travelling in a carriage with Dr. Mortimer and Henry Baskerville - Watson gives us a clear depiction of Baskerville Hall. He says:

> The avenue opened into a broad expanse of turf, and the house lay before us. In the fading light I could see that the centre was a heavy block of building from which a porch projected. The whole front was draped in ivy, with a patch clipped bare here and there where a window or coat of arms broke through the dark veil. From this central block rose the twin towers, ancient, crenelated and pierced with many loopholes. A dull light shone through heavy mullioned windows, and from the high chimneys, which rose from the steep, high angled roof there sprang a single black column of smoke.[1]

Having stood before the ruins of Fowelscombe Manor I can confirm that it *IS* indeed approached by a stretch of open grass, it *DOES* too have a porch projecting from the centre, it *IS* entirely covered by ivy, there *ARE* twin towers, they *ARE* crenelated, and the chimneys *ARE* steep. All of which shows that Conan Doyle's research was quite thorough, helping to give the reader a sense that the landscape and world they had entered was real. In fact the vividness of his descriptions have a cinematic quality which our imaginations can easily visualize.

I alluded earlier to Conan Doyle's achievement in building up an atmosphere of simmering terror in the story. He did this by employing a masterful technique at key moments in the narrative. This involved using light and darkness to create dramatic effects in much the same way as an experienced artist uses his palette to portray the shadows and highlights in a painting. One could argue that the whole of *The Hound of the Baskervilles* can be read as a battle between the dark forces of primordial evil and the bright shining light of scientific progress.

This clever play on light is delightfully demonstrated in Chapter 9, when a terrified Watson and Henry Baskerville are out tracking the escaped convict and murderer Selden. In the heavy black of night they cross the moor armed with revolvers towards Cleft Tor, where they believe he is hiding. In the distance Watson spies a small flickering light and describes it with a keen eye. He says:

> There is nothing so deceptive as the distance of a light upon a pitch-dark night, and sometimes the glimmer seemed to be far away upon the horizon and sometimes

it might have been within a few yards of us. But at last we could see whence it came, and then we knew that we were indeed very close. A guttering candle was stuck in a crevice of the rocks...Over the rocks, in the crevice of which the candle burned, there was thrust out an evil yellow face, a terrible animal face, all seamed and scored with vile passions. Foul with mire, with a bristling beard and hung with matted hair, it might well have belonged to one of those old savages who dwelt in the burrows on the hillsides.

This is just one of several dramatic episodes in this chapter using light and shade to great effect. Seldon the convict is startled by their appearance and he dashes off across the moor, where he quickly disappears from view over the brow of a hill. Watson and Sir Henry give chase, and pause by two rocks to catch their breaths. As Watson glances up to the horizon Conan Doyle uses the light of the moon to paint a masterful Gothic set piece:

And it was at this moment that there occurred a most strange and unexpected thing. We had risen from our rocks and were turning to go home, having abandoned the hopeless chase. The moon was low upon the right, and the jagged pinnacle of a granite tor stood up against the lower curve of its silver disc. There, outlined as black as an ebony statue on that shining background, I saw the figure of a man upon the tor...As far as I could judge, the figure was that of a tall, thin man. He stood with his legs a little separated, his arms folded, his head bowed, as if he were brooding over that enormous wilderness of peat and granite which lay before him. He might have been the very spirit of that terrible place.

How very clever the above passage is, because it creates not just a chillingly haunting scene, but it introduces a whole new fear into the plot, as to the identity, purpose, or threat that this cryptic figure now poses. Is he perhaps another escaped convict or confederate of Seldon's? Another murderer on the loose? Or as Watson's imagination fancies – some spectre of the marshes? Conan Doyle has once again intrigued his readers and ensured our curiosity will continue into the second half of the novel.

One of the other fine skills that Conan Doyle excelled in was his precise, clear and mellifluous dialogue. This is especially noticeable in the exchanges between Holmes and Watson, which are often engaging, sometimes barbed, and occasionally profound or moving. Holmes never minces his words, and despite his seemingly cold aloofness we do get to see a more human side of him in this dark saga. In Chapter 12, when he is convinced that the diabolical hell-hound may have a human accomplice, he speaks with passion and even tenderness to Watson of what he fears may happen. He says:

It is murder, Watson - refined, cold-blooded, deliberate murder. Do not ask me for particulars. My nets are closing upon him, even as his are upon Sir Henry, and with your help he is already almost at my mercy. There is but one danger which can threaten us. It is that he should strike before we are ready to do so. Another day - two at the most - and I have my case complete, but until then guard your charge as closely as ever a fond mother watched her ailing child.

When called upon to deliver the horror Conan Doyle does not disappoint us either. In one of the most hair-raising

"The Hound Of The Baskervilles"

Oil on canvas, 1997.

Copyright © artist Jonathan Barry.

scenes to come out of a novel, the appearance of the spectral beast in Chapter 14, is chillingly served up. Peering through a bank of fog Watson describes the moment:

> I sprang to my feet, my inert hand grasping my pistol, my mind paralysed by the dreadful shape which had sprung upon us from the shadows of the fog. A hound it was, an enormous coal-black hound, but not such a hound as mortal eyes have ever seen. Fire burst from its open mouth, its eyes glowed with a smouldering glare, its muzzle and hackles and dewlap were outlined in flickering flame. Never in the delirious dream of a disordered brain could anything more savage, more appalling, more hellish, be conceived than that dark form and savage face which broke upon us out of the wall of fog.

I find it impossible to describe the above scenes without making some mention of Sidney Paget, the original illustrator of *The Hound of the Baskervilles*. He was the first artist in the world to depict these episodes and I would encourage any first time reader to buy an edition that includes his artwork.

I happen to own a first edition of *The Hound of the Baskervilles* from 1902, and one of my chief pleasures in pouring through its pages is to admire the sixteen illustration plates of his scenes. His black and white pen and ink drawings are striking in their brooding Gothic overtones and enrich the reading experience considerably. Paget was the first person in the world to visualize what Holmes looked like, and it was *he* (not Conan Doyle) who gave Sherlock his deerstalker hat. Incredibly, in all sixty of Holme's adventures

Conan Doyle only ever described him as wearing "a soft felt cap". The deerstalker was entirely Paget's invention.

There has been a plethora of movies and TV adaptations over the last one hundred years. But I would certainly recommend the 1988 movie starring Jeremy Brett as Holmes, and Edward Hardwicke as Watson. It is impeccably produced, with stellar performances from the leads, and it remains faithful to the story and the novel's dialogue. And it was Brett, more than any other actor in the world, who most closely resembled Sidney Paget's facial depiction of Holmes.

In my estimation, Jeremy Brett and Edward Hardwicke were the definitive Holmes and Watson, an honour that they earned while making the superlative Granada ITV television series which ran from 1984 – 1994. Brett's intense analytical and highly idiosyncratic approach to playing the famous sleuth, and Hardwicke's equally intelligent no nonsense approach to Watson (both of them were very seasoned actors when they came to the roles) – made for a match in heaven.

Brett was the only TV and cinematic actor in the world to play Holmes in 41 of the 60 Conan Doyle stories. It remains to this day a high bar by which any aspiring Holmes actor must rate their achievements.

V

The Happy Prince
By
Oscar Wilde
(1854 – 1900)

I am often slow to use the phrase 'a literary genius' but in the case of Oscar Wilde it is the truth, the whole truth, and nothing but the truth, so help me God. The Irishman's talents were prodigious and he was possibly the only writer in the world who achieved brilliance in six major writing mediums: the novel, the play, poetry, short stories, essays, and fairy tales. Not even Shakespeare or Dickens could match this wide ranging versatility.

The Happy Prince is a most delightful children's fairy-tale filled with love, compassion, sympathy and humility. It can of course be read as an allegory of the vicissitudes of human life, but equally it is peppered throughout with a delicate understated sense of wit, that is both intelligent and probing. In every sentence of its twenty one pages we can see a twinkle in Wilde's eyes, you might even say a sparkle from his heart. It is an intensely personal story that comes straight from his soul. And although I have read it over twenty times, it still brings a tear to my eye on each occasion.

First published in 1888, the story is written in a similar style to the moral fables and fairy tales of the Brothers

Grimm or Hans Christian Andersen. But whereas their narratives hoped mainly to persuade children through fear, *The Happy Prince* hopes to influence through charm, warmth and kindness.

The storyline is as follows: in the middle of a fictional central European city (possibly of the 18th century), there stands a beautiful gold statue of a Happy Prince on a high column. He has a sapphire in each eye, and a ruby in his sword hilt, and his elevation on the pillar is so high that he can see every street and lane-way below him. He makes friends with a swallow who decides to sleep at the base of the statue's golden feet. The swallow is supposed to fly to Egypt to migrate for the winter. But the statue of the Happy Prince asks the swallow to stay a few extra days to help him give gifts to the poor people of the city. The swallow quickly develops a strong admiration for the statue, and agrees to help him give charitable offerings to the needy citizens. Within a few weeks the swallow is so enamoured with the kindness of the Happy Prince, that he decides not to return to Egypt at all, and tells the golden statue that he will stay with him forever.

A straightforward tale I hear you say? And yet, it is told with such heartfelt beauty and wisdom that it is able to speak to a much wider world audience than all the intellectual musings of Friedrich Nietzsche, Karl Marx, or Friedrich Engels (all of them contemporary philosophers of his age). Which is one of Wilde's greatest skills - his ability to reach the hearts and minds of the common man through a deceptively simple but highly intelligent prose.

Likewise, Wilde infuses his writing with a subtle undercurrent of assured humour. Take for example the scene where the swallow first decides to settle down at the feet of the statue in order to sleep:

> Just as he was putting his head under his wing a large drop of water fell on him." What a curious thing!" He cried, "there is not a single cloud in the sky, the stars are quite clear and bright, and yet it is raining. The climate in the north of Europe is really dreadful. The Reed used to like the rain, but that was merely her selfishness." Then another fell. "What is the use of a statue if it cannot keep the rain off?" he said; "I must look for a good chimney-pot," and he determined to fly away... [1]

Of course, moments later the reader discovers that the drops are in fact tears being shed by the statue. And thus begins the friendship and sympathy between the bird and the golden sculpture.

This in turn leads us to the kernel of the story. One single noun depicts the essence of the entire narrative: love. Whether it is the love between the swallow and the Happy Prince, or the romantic flirtation between the swallow and The Reed, or the tenderness between the poor seamstress mother and her son sick with fever, or the two young lovers on the balcony of the palace, - they are all celebrating the virtues of tenderness and affection. Wilde puts it very well in the words of the teenage lover to his girlfriend, who declares:

> "How wonderful the stars are," he said to her, "how wonderful is the power of love!"

For me this 'love' reaches a highpoint in the story when the Happy Prince asks the swallow to pluck out the ruby from his sword hilt, to give it to the poor seamstress so that she can help her ailing son. This scene is deftly written as the swallow flies through the open window of the seamstress's house. Wilde says:

> The boy was tossing feverishly on his bed, and the mother had fallen asleep, she was so tired. In he hopped, and laid the great ruby on the table beside the woman's thimble. Then he flew gently round the bed, fanning the boy's forehead with his wings. "How cool I feel," said the boy, "I must be getting better;" and he sank into a delicious slumber.

Much has been written of the extraordinary life of Oscar Wilde: his fame, his success, his trial, his fall from grace, and the despicable outrageous treatment of the British establishment in jailing him for simply being gay. But what is less heard about was his lifelong genuine concern for the injustices done to deprived and poor children. Even while serving out his own sentence in Wandsworth Prison and Reading Gaol, Wilde was horrified at the cruelties and appalling treatment of children that he witnessed there. When he was released in 1897 he wrote two moving letters to The Daily Chronicle newspaper outlining the maltreatment of juvenile offenders. It is hard to read these two published letters and not feel tearful at their contents. He describes one child locked in a cell for months screaming and whimpering for its mother, and he tells how the Warden of Reading Gaol was fired by the Prison Commissioners because he gave a crying child a biscuit.

"The Happy Prince"

Oil on canvas, 1997.

Copyright © artist Jonathan Barry.

It is this very real sympathy and affinity with children (including his own) that lay behind the inspiration for *The Happy Prince*. When tears run down the cheeks of the beautiful face of the golden statue - it is Oscar Wilde's own tears that we are witnessing. This is clearly demonstrated in the following scene:

> "In the square below," said the Happy Prince, "there stands a little match-girl. She has let her matches fall in the gutter, and they are all spoiled. Her father will beat her if she does not bring home some money, and she is crying. She has no shoes or stockings, and her little head is bare."

What happens next I will not spoil for the reader, except to say that the gentle statue performs an act of great self-sacrifice to help the penniless girl.

One further skill that Wilde excelled at was in his descriptive powers. His choice of adjectives and nouns to create a rich tapestry of details was second to none. The scene where the swallow describes his fond memories of Egypt to the Happy Prince is vibrant, and so appealing to our senses. He says:

> All the next day he sat on the Prince's shoulder, and told him stories of what he had seen in strange lands. He told him of the red ibises, who stand in long rows on the banks of the Nile, and catch gold fish in their beaks; of the Sphinx, who is as old as the world itself, and lives in the desert, and knows everything; of the merchants, who walk slowly by the side of their camels, and carry amber beads in their hands;

of the King of the Mountains of the Moon, who is as black as ebony, and worships a large crystal; of the great green snake that sleeps in a palm-tree, and has twenty priests to feed it with honey-cakes;

Because it is a relatively short fairy-tale most movie and TV companies have shied away from producing it. But I do recommend a very singular and moving animated cartoon made in 1974, by the Canadian movie company Potterton Productions. It is twenty minutes in length, and is superbly narrated by the great Canadian actor Christopher Plummer. It perfectly captures the soul of the story, and the music soundtrack by Ron Goodwin is quite gorgeous.

VI

Oh, Whistle, And I'll Come To You, My Lad
By
M.R. James
(1862 – 1936)

Montague Rhodes James was the foremost ghost story writer of his generation, re-inventing the genre in his own distinctive style. In the one hundred and fifty years before 1900 almost all supernatural tales were set in Gothic castles, ruined chapels or dreary graveyards. But by the time he published his first collection of uncanny adventures *Ghost Stories of an Antiquary* in 1904 – he had already broken the mould. He was the first author to place his monsters in more ordinary and contemporary settings such as hotels, beaches, libraries, gardens, - even buses, and with tremendous effect. He believed that in order to create a truly effective horror story it was necessary to achieve what he called 'a pleasing terror'.

This marvellous phrase (and what it meant) was at the core of the reason why his stories were so successful. Why 'pleasing'? Because he was convinced that all horror readers wanted to enjoy a certain cosy or pleasant safeness into which they could retreat should elements of the narrative frighten them too much. This included luring the reader into a false sense of security, by using familiar scenes or friendly objects. And why 'terror'? Because equally that same reader wants to be terrified, but only in short sharp doses – always with the sure knowledge that they can quickly slip on to the next page, where they know James will restore the predominantly 'pleasing' outcome. It is terror with a safety valve – a perfect formula.

When a friend of mine suggested to me many years back that I should begin reading James' ghost stories I started initially with *Oh, Whistle, And I'll Come To You, My Lad*. I am reluctant to admit that I was not very impressed with my first visit to its pages: I thought the title was unwieldy and awkward, and I did not like his somewhat offhand throw away phrases. But like a fine wine that you uncork every six months to enjoy its bouquet – with every new reading of the story I began to realize that James was a master craftsman of skilled writing. It is precisely these seemingly innocuous openings to his tales that are key to his gentle building up of a threatening atmosphere, and his eventual delivery of an odious shock.

Every adjective, noun and adverb is carefully thought through by James to capitalise on the building up of this tension. Indeed, it was only on my fifth or sixth reading of the text that I picked up on the very carefully placed hints in the narrative which pointed to the supernatural terror to come. Agatha Christie was one of James' favourite authors, and like her, he leaves carefully disguised clues to prepare the reader for the punch. It is a delight to discover these pointers, especially when they are delivered with a refined understated sense of dry humour. Believe me – this is not easy to achieve, and James excelled at it.

Oh, Whistle, And I'll Come To You, My Lad is one of his longer tales (coming in at about forty three pages in the 1st Edition of 1904), and this allowed him to build up the setting and atmosphere with greater attention to detail. It begins with innocent charm: a bored Professor of Ontography in England (named Professor Parkins) decides to spend some of his term holiday break visiting the seaside village of Burnstow in Suffolk, where it is his intention to improve on his golf, catch up on his reading, and do a little bit of archaeological digging. He stays at an old-fashioned hotel called the Globe Inn, where he books a twin room with two single beds, which overlooks the beach. There he strikes up an acquaintance with an elderly retired soldier called Colonel Wilson who is also holidaying in the Inn. Each day they breakfast together and in the afternoons they go down to the local links to play a round of golf.

One evening Parkins decides to walk alone along the beach to see if he can find the archaeological ruins of an old preceptory.

Sure enough he stumbles across the site, where he finds several promising grass mounds and hillocks. Finding a hole in the side of an oblong earth bank he puts his hand in – and to his amazement his fingers grasp a small mud-covered metal tube. Extricating the object from the opening he becomes excited that he may have found an archaeological find of some significance. All quite 'pleasing' so far. With darkness fast approaching he decides to makes his way back along the beach towards the Inn.

The passage that then follows is a most beautifully composed descriptive scene, in which a sense of haunting unease is built up and developed. James describes the vista:

> Bleak and solemn was the view on which he took a last look before starting homeward. A faint yellow light in the west showed the links, on which a few figures moving towards the club-house were still visible, the squat martello tower, the lights of Aldsey village, the pale ribbon of sands intersected at intervals by black wooden groynings, the dim and murmuring sea. The wind was bitter from the north, but was at his back when he set out for the Globe. He quickly rattled and clashed through the shingle and gained the sand, upon which, but for the groynings which had to be got over every few yards, the going was both good and quiet. One last look behind, to measure the distance he had made since leaving the ruined Templar's church, showed him a prospect of company on his walk, in the shape of a rather indistinct personage in the distance, who seemed to be making great efforts to catch up with him.[1]

As a book illustrator I found this description startlingly real to my imagination, and the sense of menace it conjured up quite palpable. This is the level and standard of horror writing that all authors in the genre should aspire to.

Once back in his hotel room, Professor Parkins proceeds to clean up the odd metal item and he removes the caked dirt from it – whereupon he discovers it to be an ancient whistle of some kind. He blows it...and then?

"Oh, Whistle, And I'll Come To You, My Lad "

Oil on canvas, 2009.

Copyright © artist Jonathan Barry.

Well – suffice to say that from this moment strange things begin to happen to him. Again, with perfect timing, at the instant when he blows the whistle, James introduces a stark premonition in the form of a sudden gale that hammers at his bedroom window. An alarmed Parkins exclaims:

> 'But what is this? Goodness! What force the wind can get up in a few minutes! What a tremendous gust! There! I knew that window fastening was no use! Ah! I thought so – both candles out. It is enough to tear the room to pieces.' The first thing was to get the window shut. While you might count twenty Parkins was struggling with the small casement, and felt almost as if he were pushing back a sturdy burglar, so strong was the pressure.

I mentioned earlier that James chose his words carefully, and in the above quotation he used the suggestive phrase "tear the room to pieces". Without doubt he is alluding here to the possibility that some unearthly entity may indeed later attempt to rip the room to pieces, or even slash Parkins to shreds! The thought has been planted in our minds.

Possibly one of the finest techniques that James used to illicit terror in his narratives - was his clever device of presenting children as intermediaries to describe the monster from a distance (Emily Brontë used the same mechanism in *Wuthering Heights* when Nelly Dean meets a hysterical crying shepherd boy on the road, who says he has seen the ghosts of Cathy and Heathcliff). A wailing child that is half frightened out of its wits is far more effective than any adult trying to describe a supernatural occurrence. It has the added bonus too of a child having a colourful imagination, and leaving us the reader questioning the validity of their sighting.

For example, the day after Parkins has blown the whistle (and having spent a sleepless night filled with nightmares) both he and Colonel Wilson once again have an enjoyable afternoon on the golf course before wandering back to the hotel. This time they are stopped in their tracks by a collision with a young lad. James describes the action:

> As they turned the corner of the house, the Colonel was almost knocked down by a boy who rushed into him at the very top of his speed, and then, instead of running away, remained hanging on to him and panting. Inquiries were useless at first. When the boy got his breath he began to howl, and still clung to the Colonel's legs. He was at last detached, but continued to howl. 'What in the world is the matter with you? What have you been up to? What have you seen?' said the two men. 'Ow, I seen it wive at me out of the winder,' wailed the boy, 'and I don't like it.' 'What window?' said the irritated Colonel. 'Come, pull yourself together, my boy.' 'The front winder it was, at the 'otel,' said the boy.

From this point on Professor Parkins realizes that the window in question was in fact his own bedroom window, and a genuine anticipation of dread starts to creep up on him as he prepares to spend his final night at the Inn. In these penultimate passages of the story James treats us to a tour de force of imminent pending abhorrence. Key to this is the increasingly claustrophobic atmosphere that causes Parkins to doubt his own senses and sanity Tossing and turning in his bed he is woken by peculiar sounds in the shaded part of his hotel room:

> For some minutes he lay and pondered over the possibilities; then he turned over sharply, and with all his eyes open lay breathlessly listening. There had been a movement, he was sure, in the empty bed on the opposite side of the room. Tomorrow he would have it moved, for there must be rats or something playing about in it. It was quiet now. No! the commotion began again. There was a rustling and shaking; surely more than any rat could cause.

And as I have no desire to spoil the pleasure of the truly gruesome monster that reveals itself to the aspiring bookworm – I will simply finish by saying that it is worth the wait, as you are never likely to forget what James conjures up. When I first read it – it made my skin crawl and I was not inclined to sleep for several days after. It is a unique creation in the annals of horror writing, and it is the monster's face in particular that will remain lodged in your imagination for a lifetime. If your curiosity is roused – do not say I didn't warn you!

Easily the best adaptation of this story, is the 1968 BBC TV production, called "Whistle and I'll Come to You", directed by Jonathan Millar, and starring the excellent Sir Michael Hordern, who plays a perfectly uptight Professor Parkins. The close-up of the camera on Hordern's terrified eyes in the final shot still packs a powerful punch today.

VII

Great Expectations
By
Charles Dickens
(1812 – 1870)

Great Expectations is one of the finest novels of the nineteenth century, rich in colourful characters, and possessing a plot with more twists and turns than a monkey puzzle. It delights, it surprises, it shocks, it hurts, and it heals. Deep within its pages runs the entire gamut of human emotions and experience, dealing bravely as it does with life, death, love, hate, courage, cowardice, marriage, separation, hope, despair, and of course what it declares in its title - expectations, and their inevitable disappointments. But it is a story full of heart and humanity, finding light in the darkest of places. Only Charles Dickens could have written it, and it marks an epoch in his maturity as a writer.

As it is such a long novel I feel it would be helpful here to give a brief summary of some (not all) of the basic plot pillars of the story. This will in no way ruin the experience for the first time literary adventurer as I will refrain from not giving out any major revelations - it will simply help to understand why I have chosen certain passages to focus on. Remember - *Great Expectations* is a work that must be finished to the last page, and read from cover to cover, otherwise the sometimes complicated plot will make no sense at all.

First published in 1861, the story is about an orphan boy called Pip who has lost both his parents and five of his brothers (we are not told how) roughly in the year 1812. He ends up living with his only surviving elder sister Mrs. Joe Gargary who marries a local blacksmith called Joe Gargary. They live in a small wooden house next to a forge near the marshes of the River Thames in Kent. They are poor uneducated people.

As a boy Pip has two strange experiences which have a profound effect on the rest of his life. Firstly, while visiting the graves of his parents on a dark bitterly cold Christmas Eve he is ambushed in the graveyard by an escaped convict who is starving and manacled. He demands that Pip bring him food, drink, and a file the next morning or he will kill him. Terrified to disobey Pip runs back to his house and secretly steals a pork pie, some brandy, and a file, and early at dawn the next day sneaks back to the convict and gives him the items. The convict (whose name is Magwitch) thanks Pip, and allows him to return unharmed to his home. The next day several British redcoat soldiers recapture Magwitch on the marshes and he is sent on a prison ship to Australia.

One year after that dramatic event Pip then receives a mysterious invitation to visit Satis House, a decaying half abandoned Gothic mansion which is inhabited by a local eccentric old spinster called Miss Havisham. She is said to be very wealthy and powerful in the nearby community, and she specifically invites Pip to go to her mansion to play there. Neither Pip or his sister or his brother-in-law know why Pip has been singled out to visit Miss Havisham. But when he gets to Satis House Miss Havisham asks Pip to play daily with an adopted girl called Estella who lives in the house with her.

Estella is very pretty, proud and arrogant, and Pip develops a crush on her. For the next few years Pip continues to visit Miss Havisham regularly, and his feelings for Estella grow stronger. Then when he becomes a teenager Pip starts his apprenticeship as a blacksmith with Joe Gargary. Four years into this apprenticeship Pip receives a letter from a solicitor telling him he has inherited a large regular income from a secret wealthy benefactor (who remains unidentified), and that Pip is to become a gentleman in London. Thus begins Pip's coming-of-age adventures and his many varied expectations, aspirations and disappointments along his journey. But the entire novel remains an absolutely engrossing tale filled with intrigue, which keeps us guessing until the very end.

Many critics have described *Great Expectations* as one part Gothic Thriller, and one part Tragic Romance, interspersed here and there with some fine comic caricatures. This I feel is an accurate depiction of what the book has to offer, as Dickens was a master of them all. Right from the first chapter he has us on the edge of our seats.

You will rarely find a more powerful opening scene to a novel as the sudden appearance of the mysterious convict Abel Magwitch in Chapter 1, when he accosts a terrified Pip in the graveyard:

'Hold your noise!' cried a terrible voice, as a man started up from among the graves at the side of the church porch. 'Keep still, you little devil, or I'll cut your throat!' A fearful man, all in course gray, with a great iron on his leg. A man with no hat, and with broken shoes, and with an old rag tied round his head. A man who had been soaked in water, and smothered in mud, and lamed by stones, and cut by flints, and stung by nettles, and torn by briars; who limped, and shivered, and glared and growled; and whose teeth chattered in his head as he seized me by the chin.[1]

Dickens' real genius lay in the creation of unforgettable characters with names that perfectly matched their personalities. He gave the world hundreds of the most famous literary characters of all time, and *Great Expectations* is no exception. Magwitch for example, is just one of a whole raft of wonderfully named individuals in the story, including: Pip, Miss Havisham, Joe Gargary, Mrs. Joe Gargary, Estella, Uncle Pumblechook, Herbert Pocket, Clara, Mrs. Hubble, Mr. Wopsle, Biddy, Mr. Jaggers, John Wemmick, Bentley Drummle, The Aged Parent, Molly, Compeyson, and the delightfully odious Dolge Orlick. Can't you just visualize each one of them before even reading a single word of the text?

Without doubt one of the most memorable and haunted souls ever to come from Dickens' imagination is Miss Havisham. She is a dysfunctional reclusive old spinster who lives locked up in her crumbling Georgian pile, where she sits in darkness every day shutting out the light and life of the world. Abandoned by her fiancé on her wedding day, she

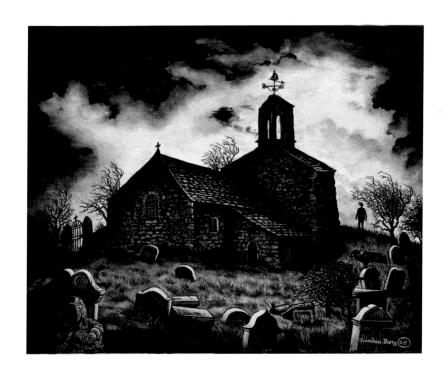

"Magwich"

Oil on canvas, 1993.

Copyright © artist Jonathan Barry.

has turned inward and bitter, and sits alone in her faded and torn wedding dress, stuck in a moment of trauma that holds her an emotional prisoner.

In Chapter 8, Pip meets her for the first time, and on entering the dark chamber where she languishes, he gives us a striking description. He says:

In an armchair, with an elbow resting on the table and her head leaning on that hand, sat the strangest lady I have ever seen, or shall ever see. She was dressed in rich materials - satins, and lace, and silks - all of white. Her shoes were white. And she had a long white veil dependent from her hair, and she had bridal flowers in her hair, but her hair was white. Some bright jewels sparkled on her neck and on her hands, and some other jewels lay sparkling on the table. She had not quite finished dressing, for she had but one shoe on - the other was on the table near her hand - her veil was but half arranged, her watch and chain were not put on....I saw that the bride within the bridal dress had withered like the dress, and like the flowers, and had no brightness left but the brightness of her sunken eyes.

Dickens does not reveal the reasons why Miss Havisham behaves this way, nor her motives or reasons for doing things, until near the end of the story. But throughout the novel she is the central pivot around which the entire plot rotates.

There was a concerted cynical movement amongst certain reviewers in the 20th century who tried to pour scorn on Dickens' ability to write effective romance. Not only is this ludicrous - but in *Great Expectations* more than in any of his other works, Dickens displays a deep understanding of human love, and the complexities and frailty of that emotion. Who can read Pip's passionate and gut-wrenching declaration of love to Estella in Chapter 44, without shedding a tear? I know I did. It is a tender speech of heartfelt intensity. Pip exclaims:

"You are part of my existence, part of myself. You have been in every line I have read, since I first came here, the rough common boy whose poor heart you wounded even then. You have been in every prospect I have ever seen since —on the river, on the sails of the ships, on the marshes, in the clouds, in the light, in the darkness, in the wind, in the woods, in the sea, in the streets. You have been the embodiment of every graceful fancy that my mind has ever become acquainted with... Estella, to the last hour of my life, you cannot choose but remain part of my character, part of the little good in me, part of the evil."

Neither was Dickens afraid to extemporize on the merits of friendship and kindness. These were virtues close to his own heart through good times and bad. When Pip gets badly sick in Chapter 57, it is his brother-in-law Joe Gargary who nurses him back to health. It's a charming and tender scene full of human compassion and decency. As he recovers from the delirium of his fever Pip thanks Joe profusely with tears in his eyes, declaring:

'Oh, Joe, you break my heart! Look angry at me, Joe. Strike me, Joe. Tell me of my ingratitude. Don't be so good to me!' For Joe had actually laid his head down on the pillow at my side and put his arm round my neck, in his joy that I knew him.

As a perfect accompaniment to the book, I would highly recommend watching the 1946 movie of *Great Expectations,* directed by David Lean. This is the greatest movie adaptation ever made of a Dickens novel, and it is a cinematic masterpiece. John Mills is magnificent as Pip, and he is superbly supported by Finlay Currie as Magwitch, Alex Guinness as Herbert Pocket, and Martita Hunt as Miss Havisham.

VIII

Dracula

By
Bram Stoker
(1847 – 1912)

Dracula is the most famous horror story ever written, and is considered by many to be the greatest vampire tale of all time. It is a world cultural phenomenon and has entered the record books as one of the most filmed stories on the planet, second only to the Sherlock Holmes franchise. Since it was first published in 1897 its influence on literature, movies, television, Halloween festivals, and iconography is unparalleled. And the fact that it was written by a modest Protestant from the suburb of Clontarf in Dublin - Bram Stoker - should make all Irish people feel especially proud.

Anything that has enjoyed so much success and spawned so many clichés must surely be overrated and a poor read - right? Wrong! It is a marvellous novel that has lost none of its terror or capacity to shock. *Dracula* is a genuine Gothic thriller and like a fine wine it gets better and better with every passing year. Bram wrote twelve novels of varying quality, but this is his best. I myself have read it countless times and each journey through its pages uncovers fresh evidence of Stoker's skills as a master of the macabre.

On what do I base this claim? There are several pertinent reasons to enjoy it. Firstly, Stoker's forensic research into the customs, folklore, history, geography and superstitions of Transylvania are used to great effect to establish a convincing setting for the opening four chapters of the book. He spent ten long years researching for the story, and this hard work paid off. The reader quite literally believes they are travelling in a caleche through the snow-capped peaks of the Carpathian Mountains, such is Stoker's attention to detail.

Secondly, one of Bram's greatest strengths as a writer is his superb descriptive powers, especially in depicting the majestical views of mountains, forests, castles, rivers, ravines, seascapes and graveyards. Without wishing to exaggerate, it is my genuine opinion that he was, and remains, the finest geographical descriptive author of his age.

Thirdly, Stoker created the greatest villain in the annals of horror - Count Dracula.

Why is he the greatest? Because this vampire has more supernatural powers at his disposal than any other monster in the history of literature. He has the strength of 20 men, can change shape into a dog, bat, wolf or mist, he can command animals such as wolves and rats to do his bidding, he is able to manipulate the weather including storms and fog banks, he can hypnotize and mind read, and long before Darth Vader was using The Force, Stoker gave the Count his own Force, whereby he can hurl people and objects across rooms with one sweep of his imperious hand.

"The Borgo Pass"

Oil on canvas, 1997.

Copyright © artist Jonathan Barry.

Fourthly, like all classic novels *Dracula* contains some hair-raising passages that are uniquely original, powerful, and cinematic in quality.

Having illustrated several versions of *Dracula* in my career as an artist and book illustrator, I travelled to Transylvania many years back to prepare my research before drawing or painting any scenes from the text. The purpose of my trip was to retrace the footsteps of Jonathan Harker's Journal (at the beginning of the novel) on exactly the same dates that he travelled through the Carpathians from 3rd May - 30th June.

I arrived in Bucharest in early May 1990, and visited Bran Castle, Tirgoviste, Lake Snagov, Brasov, and the Birgau Pass (which actually exists). I was amazed at Stoker's accuracy of the geographical landscape and indeed I was convinced he must have spent several months there taking notes. But we now know that he never visited Transylvania at all. Instead he gathered all his source material from his research at the British Museum in London and while studying at The Whitby Library in Yorkshire.

As I stood at the base of Bran Castle I read aloud Stoker's description of Castle Dracula in Chapter 3. He says:

> The castle was built on the corner of a great rock, so that on three sides it was quite impregnable, and great windows were placed here where sling, or bow, or culverin could not reach. To the west was a great valley, and then, rising far away, great jagged mountain fastnesses, rising peak on peak, the sheer rock studded with mountain ash and thorn. [1]

I can confirm that Bran Castle IS indeed impregnable from three sides - I know, because I was there. And there IS a great valley to the west of it, and with my own eyes I saw copious amounts of mountain ash and thorn surrounding the castle walls.

Likewise, I saw and experienced so many of the details that Jonathan Harker describes in the first four chapters: including the lovely blossom of the cherry trees, the carpets of bluebells at the borders of the woodlands, the heavy leiter wagons used by peasant farmers (which still exist in parts of rural Romania today). I even eat both the 'impletata' and 'robber steak' that Harker mentions in Chapter I. What's my point? That Stoker's research was meticulous, and his attention to detail makes us the reader really believe in the story's location and physical world.

I have already alluded to Count Dracula's ability to hurl people and objects using a magical force. One terrific example of this is when the three female vampires that share the castle with him, attempt to seduce Jonathan Harker by biting into his neck. Just as they are ready to sink their fangs into Harker's throat, a jealous Count bursts into the room and unleashes his wrath upon them. Harker describes what happens:

> I was conscious of the presence of the Count, and of his being as if lapped in a storm of fury. His eyes were positively blazing. The red light in them was lurid, as if the flames of hell-fire blazed behind them. With a fierce sweep of his arm,

"Castle Dracula"

Oil on canvas, 1994.

he hurled the woman from him, and then motioned to the others, as though he were beating them back; it was the same imperious gesture that I had seen used to the wolves.

Not even Voldemort in *Harry Potter* or Saruman in *The Lord of the Rings* have this inestimable power in their arsenal of supernatural weapons. It makes the Count unique.

All classic novels that stand the test of time contain certain famous scenes that once read - can never be forgotten. *Dracula* shines in this category, and surely one of the most frightening passages ever to be published is the staking of Lucy Westenra. In Chapter 16, Van Helsing, along with Dr. Seward, Arthur Holmwood, and Quincey Morris, all enter the tomb where she lies, with the express intention of staking her through the heart to release her from the throes of being 'Un-Dead'.

It is a gripping scene full of direst tension. As the stake enters her breast Stoker describes the carnage:

> The Thing in the coffin writhed; and a hideous, blood-curdling screech came from the opened red lips. The body shuck and quivered and twisted in wild contortions; the sharp white teeth champed together till the lips were cut and the mouth was smeared with a crimson foam. But Arthur never faulted. He looked like a figure of Thor as his untrembling arm rose and fell, driving deeper and deeper the mercy-bearing stake, whilst the blood from the pierced heart welled and spurted up around it.

The pace and rhythm of Stoker's prose is immaculate here, offering one of many visual treats that would attract so many movie directors in the next one hundred years. When it came to thrilling rapid action sequences, Bram was as good as Robert Louis Stevenson, or H. Rider Haggard.

I am sure you have often heard the phrase - "What's in a name?" In the case of this book - everything. It is hard to believe that for almost eight of the years that Bram had been working on the text, he used the working title of 'Count Wampyr'. Then just one year before he gave the final draft to his publisher he changed the working title of the novel to 'The Undead'. In fact, just six weeks before the book was published in May 1897, he handed in his final typescript to Archibald Constable & Co (his publisher) still bearing the name of 'The Undead' in Bram's own handwriting on the title page (incidently I possess a photocopy of this title page and Stoker's handwriting was terrible). Amazingly, someone in Constable & Co. convinced him during these six weeks to rename the book *Dracula*. Bram relented, ditching the not so memorable title 'The Undead' and the brilliant, eye-catching, pithy name of *Dracula* was agreed upon.

Thank God for us the reading public that such a change was made. Can you imagine how different literary history may have been had the story hit the bookshops called 'The Undead'? It would likely have attracted only modest attention. But *Dracula?* - that was a stroke of genius.

When you have finished reading the book I do recommend one TV adaptation made by the BBC in 1977. It starred Louis Jordan as the Count, with Frank Finlay as an excellent

Van Helsing. Jordan gives a fine sensuous performance, portraying a highly intelligent aristocratic overlord. This version for the most part kept faithfully to the dialogue and plot of the novel. But if you are determined to watch a movie – you will not be disappointed with the credible 1958 Hammer classic starring the superlative Christopher Lee in the title role.

IX

The Strange Case of Dr. Jekyll and Mr. Hyde

By
Robert Louis Stevenson
(1850 – 1894)

Robert Louis Stevenson yearned to be a writer – it was in his blood, and nothing on God's earth was going to stop him achieving that goal. Despite a short life of only 44 years in which he was constantly in poor health and in considerable physical pain – he was possessed of an almost super human willpower that drove him on to become one of the greatest writers of the 19th century. Along with half a dozen other authors of the Victorian era – he was an undoubted literary genius of impeccable writing skills.

Born in Edinburgh in 1850, he was already an acclaimed novelist, a world celebrity, an accomplished poet, a travel writer, an intrepid adventurer, and a fully qualified lawyer – all this by his 33rd birthday. He wrote several masterpieces (usually when he was bedridden) that would shine as standard bearers in several important literary genres: including the sea adventure novel, the historical romance novel, and the horror novel.

One of those seminal works was *The Strange Case of Dr. Jekyll and Mr. Hyde,* a powerful introspective novella, first published in 1886, dealing with the struggles of the human soul, and the constant battle between good and evil in all human beings. Dr. Jekyll himself summed up the essence of the plot succinctly in his statement at the end of the tale, when he says: "Man is not truly one, but truly two".

Miraculously, Stevenson wrote the book in just three days from his sickbed, where he was nursed back to health by his American wife Fanny Osbourne. It was the first story of its kind in horror fiction, in which a man could turn himself physically into his evil alter ego by taking a concoction of drugs. It spawned hundreds of movies and television adaptations (some of which we rightly laugh at today for their lack of sophistication), but in 1886 it caused a sensation, and rightly so.

Throughout the text Stevenson displays his flawless skills as a storyteller. It is beautifully written in confident nuanced prose, with excellent pacing, and a buoyant cadence in the descriptive passages. Anyone who aspires to be a writer will ignore Robert Louis Stevenson at their peril. Everything he created demands and deserves repeated reading.

The narrative broadly follows these lines: Dr. Jekyll is a highly respected doctor who lives in a wealthy house in Cavendish Square in London, and is much loved both by his patients, servants, friends and neighbours. But unbeknown to them he lives a double life. Discovering a concoction of chemicals and compounds in his scientific laboratory – he drinks this mixture each night and transforms himself into Mr. Hyde – his evil other half. Thus, by day he lives a perfectly civilised existence as a doctor, while by night he lives a life of

"Mr. Hyde's Bloody Deeds"

Oil on canvas, 2009.

Copyright © artist Jonathan Barry.

depravity and corruption. Believing he will never be caught Jekyll continues with this deception, until something goes badly wrong.

Stevenson was a master at setting a mood, and his descriptions of Victorian London with its dark decrepit gaslit laneways, and ramshackle slums creates an atmosphere of reeking doom. Take for example his fine vivid depiction of a conspicuous building in Chapter 1:

> Two doors from one corner, on the left hand going east, the line was broken by the entry of a court; and just at that point, a certain sinister block of building thrust forward its gable on the street. It was two storeys high; showed no window, nothing but a door on the lower storey and a blind forehead of discoloured wall on the upper; and bore in every feature the marks of prolonged and sordid negligence. The door, which was equipped with neither bell nor knocker, was blistered and distained. Tramps slouched into the recess and struck matches on the panels; children kept shop upon the steps; the schoolboy had tried his knife on the mouldings; and for close on a generation, no one had appeared to drive away these random visitors or to repair their ravages.[1]

In the above passage Stevenson already has us hooked with curiosity as to what is behind that door, and we feel most nervous.

We are not told specifically in the narrative as to the exact particulars of Mr. Hyde's nightly crimes – it is left mainly to our imaginations. But when he is occasionally caught in the act we are certainly made to shudder. Again in Chapter

1, when Mr. Enfield describes to Mr. Utterson (one of Dr.Jekyll's closest friends) his first encounter with Hyde we get a real taste of his deadly capabilities. Enfield describes the circumstances:

> All at once, I saw two figures: one a little man who was stumping along eastward at a good walk. And the other a girl of maybe eight or ten who was running as hard as she was able down a cross street. Well, sir, the two ran into one another naturally enough at the corner; and then came the horrible part of the thing; for the man trampled calmly over the child's body and left her screaming on the ground. It sounds nothing to hear, but it was hellish to see.

A theme that was central to all Stevenson's novels (even in his supernatural tales) was the loyalty of friends, and the honour that these gentlemen prized amongst each other. In the frantic and often cold lifestyle of the 21st century such quaint ideals may seem strange to us. But it is hard to read certain passages in this novella and not feel touched by these sentiments. In Stevenson's own lifetime friends were quite literally willing to die for each other – such was the bond between them. So when Dr. Lanyon invites Mr. Utterson into his dining room in chapter 2, we read:

> At sight of Mr. Utterson, he sprang up from his chair and welcomed him with both hands. The geniality, as was the way of the man, was somewhat theatrical to the eye; but it reposed on genuine feeling. For these two were old friends, old mates both at school and college, both thorough respecters of themselves and of each other, and, what does

not always follow, men who thoroughly enjoyed each other's company.

As Mr. Hyde grows more reckless with each crime – his excesses become more pronounced until they reach a peak in Chapter 4, with the murder of Sir Danvers Carew. This is a superb piece of writing, thrilling with exquisite tension and electric violence. The murder is witnessed by a maid-servant who sees it acted out in the laneway below her window. Addressed by a kindly old gentleman who wishes Hyde a pleasant evening, the cloaked brute unleashes his barely repressed boiling hatred. Stevenson describes the malevolence:

> He had in his hand a heavy cane, with which he was trifling; but he answered never a word, and seemed to listen with an ill-contained impatience. And then all of a sudden he broke out in a great flame of anger, stamping with his foot, brandishing the cane, and carrying on (as the maid described it) like a madman. The old gentleman took a step back, with an air of one very much surprised and a trifle hurt; and at that Mr. Hyde broke out of all bounds, and clubbed him to the earth. And next moment, with ape-like fury, he was trampling his victim under foot, and hailing down a storm of blows, under which the bones were audibly shattered and the body jumped upon the roadway. At the horror of these sights and sounds, the maid fainted.

It will be noticed that I have not explained what goes *wrong* in Dr. Jekyll's secret dual existence, nor will I tell how the tale ends – these are both delights that the reader should be allowed to savour over a glass of wine and a roaring fire. Stevenson keeps us guessing right to the end. Even when Poole (Dr. Jekyll's butler) calls at Mr. Utterson's house pleading with him to come back to Cavendish Row (because he suspects some danger has befallen his Master) we are still unclear as to what has happened to Dr. Jekyll or his alter ego inside the confines of the locked laboratory.

Easily my favourite scene in the story is that which follows – when a fearful Mr. Utterson and a depressed Poole cross the desolate streets of London. It is a singularly haunting and foreboding passage rich in the prose of a master wordsmith. For a book illustrator or artist it is a treat for the visual eye. Stevenson paints the scene:

> It was a wild, cold, seasonable night of March, with a pale moon, lying on her back as though the wind had tilted her, and a flying wrack of the most diaphanous and lawny texture. The wind made talking difficult, and flecked the blood into the face. It seemed to have swept the streets unusually bare of passengers, besides; for Mr. Utterson thought he had never seen that part of London so deserted. He could have wished it otherwise; never in his life had he been conscious of so sharp a wish to see and touch his fellow-creatures; for, struggle as he might, there was borne in upon his mind a crushing anticipation of calamity. The square, when they got there, was all full of wind and dust, and the thin trees in the garden were lashing themselves along the railing.

During the 20th century, there have been several excellent movie productions brought to the silver screen. One that has stood the test of time is the silent classic from 1920 called 'Dr. Jekyll and Mr. Hyde', starring the incomparable John Barrymore. Regarded by many film critics as one of America's finest actors, Barrymore gives a heady performance. In his initial transfiguration scene where he changes from Dr. Jekyll into Mr. Hyde, he did this in one take, using no make-up, but by contorting his face and body into extraordinary convulsions. To this day it is an utterly compelling and deeply disturbing scene.

X

Alice's Adventures in Wonderland
By
Lewis Carroll
(1832 – 1898)

Lewis Carroll was a great writer, a respected mathematician, a pioneering photographer (he took over 3,000 photographic plates), an Anglican Deacon, a teacher, and a humorist quite ahead of his time. He excelled in all of these areas, and we can find elements of each of these skills in his most famous creation *Alice's Adventures In Wonderland*. It remains one of the most famous books in the world with a legacy and influence on western culture that is breathtaking. Since it was first published in 1865 it has been translated into 97 languages, has spawned hundreds of movies, TV adaptations, radio broadcasts and plays, and is on the syllabus of universities and colleges worldwide.

Its characters and fantasy world have been turned into a myriad of commercial products including theme parks, porcelain figurines, tea sets, china ware, greeting cards, biscuit tins, Easter eggs, stationary, calendars, – even cuddly toys. We should not forget that Carroll was deaf in one ear, had a stammer, was bullied in school, and walked awkwardly with a knee injury that he sustained in childhood. All of these physical infirmities helped to sharpen his wit and self-deprecating sense of humour (which he displays delightfully throughout the text). Nothing like it was ever written before or since, and it remains unique.

Part of its fascination is the utterly original, often hilarious, and sometimes baffling world that Carroll created in the story. It is a topsy-turvy children's yarn where nothing is what it seems and everything is upside down. Throughout it reads like a surreal dream, interspersed with outrageous flights of fancy – whereas in other passages it takes on an atmosphere of lurid nightmares. No wonder then that many psychologists have asserted that Lewis was on drugs when he wrote it (laudanum was widely used by writers in the 19th century – Samuel Taylor Coleridge wrote the whole of his poem *Kubla Khan* under its influence).

But I am afraid its contents were the result of a much more mundane origin. The 'silliness' at the heart of the narrative was an essential element of a literary genre that was popular in Carroll's day called 'literary nonsense'. Edmund Lear's *Book of Nonsense* and Carroll's *Alice's Adventures In Wonderland* were the two leading examples of this movement. 'Literary nonsense' was quite literally a story that threw all writing norms out the window, and focused on a tale that was ludicrous, amusing, and poked fun at the conventions of Victorian society. Everything from Britain's royal family, the judicial court system, Admirals, soldiers, the aristocracy, social etiquette, school teachers, the working classes – even Victorian theories on mathematics – they are all laughed at and ridiculed in *Alice's Adventures In Wonderland*.

"The Mad Hatter's Tea-Party"

Oil on canvas, 1999.

Copyright © artist Jonathan Barry.

How he came up with the idea is almost as fascinating as the story itself. In July 1862 Carroll (real name the Reverend Charles Dodgson) was rowing up the River Isis in Oxfordshire with his good friend The Reverend Robinson Duckworth, and they were accompanied in the boat by the three daughters of Henry Liddell. Carroll and Duckworth shared many cultural interests with Liddell, and all three men frequented each other's homes regularly. Because of this Liddell was quite happy to allow his daughters to spend many summer afternoons with the two clerics enjoying the delights of the English countryside.

The three girls were Alice, Lorina, and Edith Liddell. As they sculled up the river that day from Folly Bridge to the village of Godstow five miles away – Carroll began to tell the girls about an idea he had for a story, about a girl finding her way down a rabbit hole into a fantasy world below the ground. Alice Liddell loved the idea so much that she pleaded with Carroll to write it down. This he did – and a month later he read the girls some more of the story in a second boat trip in August. By November he handed Alice Liddell a fully completed handwritten draft to read. Not only did she love the story – but Carroll also allowed his good friend the author George MacDonald to read it, and MacDonald encouraged Carroll to show it to a publisher. The rest – as they say – is history.

It is important to remember that before this was published the only stories children could read were either the dry moralistic fairy tales of Hans Christian Andersen, or the equally rigid Aesop's fables. *Alice's Adventures In Wonderland* was the first story written specifically to make children laugh. It also portrayed the first children's heroine (Alice) who not only holds her own against all the adult or authoritative figures in the tale, but in fact is intellectually and morally superior to them. Carroll empowered all children throughout the world to believe in themselves through Alice's plucky and sensible nature. However rude or ignorant the adult individuals are that she encounters – she is never intimidated by them.

One of the standout features of the book is the exceptional number of unforgettable colourful characters. What a joy it is for any child or adult to read the book for the first time, and to be introduced to the madness of such luminaries as the White Rabbit, the Caterpillar, the Dodo, the Queen of Hearts, the Cheshire Cat, the Mad Hatter, the March Hare, Bill the Lizard, and more. It always makes me laugh when Alice tries to maintain her dignity no matter how crazy the conversations get or how strange circumstances appear to her.

In Chapter 5, (when she has magically shrunk to only three inches high) her patience is sorely tested when she is quizzed by a blue caterpillar sitting on the top of a mushroom:

> The Caterpillar and Alice looked at each other for some time in silence: at last the Caterpillar took the hookah out of its mouth, and addressed her in a languid, sleepy voice. "Who are you?" said the Caterpillar. This was not an encouraging opening for a conversation. Alice replied, rather shyly, "I – I

"Advice From A Caterpillar"

Oil on canvas, 1999.

Copyright © artist Jonathan Barry.

hardly know, Sir, just at present – at least I know who I was when I got up this morning, but I think I must have changed several times since then."[1]

A very endearing figure in the story is the White Rabbit. He is cute, cuddly, enigmatic, splendidly dressed, and children the world over adore him. The idea of a walking, talking rabbit wearing an Englishman's waistcoat with a gold pocket watch and carrying white kid gloves and a fan-has fascinated generations of young readers. Just as Alice is curious to know where the White Rabbit is going to – so too are we intrigued.

Likewise, why he keeps glancing at his pocket watch and repeating "I'm late! I'm late!" is a puzzle (indeed we don't find out until the end of the story what event it is that he is late for). His dialogue throughout the tale is deliberately evasive, and yet all children want to hug him because they know that he is troubled about something. Even Alice wants to comfort him in Chapter 4, when she sees him approaching:

> It was the White Rabbit, trotting slowly back again, and looking anxiously about as it went, as if it had lost something; and she heard it muttering to itself "The Duchess! The Duchess! Oh my dear paws! Oh my fur and whiskers! She'll get me executed, as sure as ferrets are ferrets!"

My own favourite character is the marvellous Cheshire Cat, an oversized mischievous talking feline with a beaming mouth full of teeth, who has the power to make itself invisible. It is a precocious and eloquent creature who deliberately plays mind games with Alice by trying to tie her up in knots using riddles and double entendres. While Alice is clearly annoyed with its sarcasm she does find herself strangely drawn to the cat nonetheless. In Chapter 6, Carroll gives us a fine example:

> The Cat only grinned when it saw Alice. It looked good-natured, she thought: still it had very long claws and a great many teeth, so she felt that it ought to be treated with respect. "Would you tell me, please, which way I ought to go from here?" "That depends a good deal on where you want to get to," said the Cat. "I don't much care where – "said Alice. "Then it doesn't matter which way you go," said the Cat. "– so long as I get somewhere," Alice added as an explanation. "Oh, you're sure to do that," said the Cat, "if you only walk long enough."

A most surreal scene in the story comes in Chapter 8, when Alice finds her way onto a croquet-ground where three human sized cards (from a pack of cards) are painting a bush of white roses with red paint. Despite the fact that their bodies are playing cards – they all three have heads, arms, and legs, and each of them is carrying a pot of red paint with matching paint brush. The great artist Salvador Dali (himself a Master of Surrealism) was apparently tickled pink by this episode, and I can understand why.

When Dali illustrated his own version of *Alice's Adventures In Wonderland* in 1969, he featured this scene strongly in his artwork. It appealed to the sublime in his imagination, just as it does to mine. Carroll describes it tongue-in-cheek:

"I'm Late"

Oil on canvas, 1999.

Copyright © artist Jonathan Barry.

A large rose-tree stood near the entrance of the garden: the roses growing on it were white, but there were three gardeners at it, busily painting them red. Alice thought this a very curious thing, and she went nearer to watch them, and just as she came up to them she heard one of them say, "Look out now, Five! Don't go splashing paint over me like that!" "I couldn't help it," said Five, in a sulky tone; "Seven jogged my elbow."

It would be most remiss of me not to mention the importance of John Tenniel's famous illustrations to the success of the book since it was first published in 1865. Tenniel was the first illustrator of *Alice's Adventures In Wonderland,* and he was the first person in the world to visualize what Alice and the other characters look like. Amazingly, nowhere in the story does Carroll attempt to describe either what Alice looks like (facially or otherwise) or the clothes that she wears. It was John Tenniel who decided roughly what age to make Alice, what type of garments to give her, her hairstyle, and even her style of shoes. Significantly, it was he who gave her the famous frock and braided petticoat that she has forever been associated with. All illustrators since 1865 have been influenced by his images (myself included) and we owe him a grateful recognition to the visual importance he played in bringing Alice to life, along with all of the other characters.

When you have finished giggling at Alice's madcap adventures – do make sure to watch the equally funny Disney animated cartoon movie from 1951. Despite its slight Americanisation of Alice's character it is a magnificent realisation of Carroll's imagination, and perfectly captures the idiosyncratic madness of the story. Through the inspired use of such brilliant voice-over artists as Ed Wynn (as the Mad Hatter), Sterling Holloway (the Cheshire Cat), and Verna Felton (the Queen of Hearts) Disney made Carroll's amazing dialogue sing. It is a visually stunning movie, artistically accomplished, and downright hilarious.

XI

A Christmas Carol

By

Charles Dickens

(1812 – 1870)

A Christmas Carol is the most famous Christmas story ever written, and it is also a very fine ghostly tale. It is the best and most accomplished of all Dickens' creations – and ranks as a timeless classic. Every author in the world wishes that they had written it, and it is a landmark of literary history. The book made famous several of what are now entrenched Christmas traditions, including: family gatherings, seasonal food and drink, dancing, games, forgiveness, charitable works, and a spirit of goodwill towards all men. It is even credited by many literary historians as having established the phrase "Merry Christmas" (although this is more difficult to prove definitively). It is an incredible accomplishment for any story to have achieved this deep-set influence and iconography, and it was Dickens' crowning glory in a very rich literary career.

Who today in western civilisation, almost two hundred years after its publication, can sit down to a Christmas dinner, and not think of the prize Turkey that Scrooge buys and sends to Bob Cratchit and Tiny Tim, or not salivate at Dickens' glorious depictions of food, or not delight at the welcome sound of church bells ringing in the Christmas morning (similar to those outside Scrooge's counting-house), or not feel nostalgic for the singing of Christmas carols by children in mufflers (immortalised by the boy who attempts to sing a carol to Scrooge), or not want to make up with a family member that we may have fallen out with (as Scrooge does with his nephew Fred), or give a donation to a well-deserved charity? The reach of this tale is long, *very* long – and *A Christmas Carol* forever remains in our subconscious memory.

At this point I am going to put my head on the block and admit that I am unashamedly in love with this classic. But before I wax lyrical as to its literary merits (which are many) I would like to talk a little bit about the extraordinary circumstances surrounding the publication of the first edition, not least because it almost permanently ruined Dickens financially. It is an incredible fact that Dickens wrote the text in just six weeks, between October to December 1843. It is said that in the months before he started writing it he walked fifteen to twenty miles every night through the streets of London to collect source material. He needed *A Christmas Carol* to be a success that year, because *Martin Chuzzlewit* had failed to engage the public's affection earlier that summer and was a financial flop.

In fact, Chapman & Hall his publisher had cut his income and imposed stricter conditions on his contract, putting Dickens under pressure. This goes some way to explaining why Dickens decided to agree with Chapman & Hall that he (Dickens himself) would agree to publish it at his own

"Humbug!"

Oil on canvas, 1996.

Copyright © artist Jonathan Barry.

expense, in exchange for a certain percentage of the realised profits. He did so, insisting on having gold gilt edges, and gold gilt titles to the front cover and spine in the 1st Edition of 19th December 1843, and printing it in hardback. Despite the initial immediate success of this 1st edition of 6,000 copies selling out in just five days before Christmas Eve 1843 – Dickens was to make a financial loss on it, earning just £940 pounds from the sales by the end of 1844 – not enough to recuperate his printing costs.

He compounded this error by taking another ill-judged decision just weeks after Christmas 1843, when he decided to sue Parley's Illustrated Library, who had brought out and published an unauthorised version of *A Christmas Carol* in early January 1844, without Dickens' prior knowledge or consent. Consequently, in that same month Dickens sued them and won, but Parley declared themselves bankrupt, and Dickens had to pay out £700 pounds in costs (a very sizeable sum of money then).

In fact, in his lifetime Dickens only made modest returns from the sales of the book - it was mainly by doing reading performances of the story that he managed to procure a real profit. He did one hundred and twenty seven of these live readings from 1853 until 1870 (when he passed away). All of the above makes it ironic that despite these setbacks the book still went on to become a universal and perennial hit, discovered and rediscovered by generation after generation of new readers. Why was is it to become so popular?

Because it is a perfect story – yes perfect. Of all the other tales that I have discussed in this book none could be claimed to be entirely perfect – but *A Christmas Carol* is just so. Its chief literary merits are: assured composition, some of the most memorable characters ever created, adroit pacing, a convincing and well executed (albeit slightly romantic) plot, a sublime rendition of Gothic horror and atmosphere, gentle understated humour, genuine heartfelt humanity, and the most convincing case ever penned by a writer: that there remains in all of us a chance at redemption.

From its first sentence Dickens never puts a foot wrong. "Marley was dead to begin with" is the brilliant opening salvo, immediately making us laugh, while at the same time introducing the theme of death, and making us acutely curious to know who Marley was (we discover quickly that he is the dead business partner of Ebenezer Scrooge). Indeed, by the second page of the story Dickens already displays a vibrant confidence in his description of his main tragic character Ebenezer Scrooge. It is as if Dickens knew himself that Scrooge would become over time one of his finest literary creations. His description of the miser's face is marvellous:

> Oh! But he was a tight-fisted hand at the grindstone, Scrooge! A squeezing, wrenching, grasping, scraping, clutching, covetous, old sinner! Hard and sharp as flint, from which no steel had ever struck out generous fire; secret, and self-contained, and solitary as an oyster. The cold within him froze his old features, nipped his pointed nose, shrivelled his

cheek, stiffened his gait; made his eyes red, his thin lips blue; and spoke out shrewdly in his grating voice.[1]

We soon learn that Scrooge is despised and hated by everyone he knows for his meanness, greed, and cruel heart. He runs a dingy counting-house in the side streets of London where he employs a clerk called Bob Cratchit who he pays and treats poorly. On this particular Christmas Eve he returns home in the dark where he is visited by the ghost of his dead business partner Jacob Marley. He warns Scrooge that he will be visited by three other apparitions, who will try to convince Scrooge that he must change his greedy evil ways, or be doomed to damnation.

Without doubt the highlight of the narrative is the appearance of these three admonishing spirits. In the hands of a less experienced writer these supernatural occurrences could have been inept bordering on the mawkish – but Dickens describes each ghostly visitation so powerfully, and with such rich visual detail, that it is like looking at a Dutch masters oil painting. When the Ghost of Christmas Present (the jolly ghost) materializes in the room next to Scrooge's bedchamber, we are treated to a description of a sumptuous Christmas banquet, one that arouses in the reader all of our innate festive appetites. This passage is a riot of colour and aromas, and would make any human being pine for the sensuous delights of a Christmas feast.

Scrooge describes what he sees:

The crisp leaves of holly, mistletoe, and ivy reflected back the light, as if so many little mirrors had been scattered there; and such a mighty blaze went roaring up the chimney, as that dull petrification of a hearth had never known in Scrooge's time, or Marley's, or for many and many a winter season gone. Heaped up on the floor, to form a kind of throne, were turkeys, geese, game, poultry, brawn, great joints of meat, sucking-pigs, long wreaths of sausages, mince-pies, plum-puddings, barrels of oysters, red-hot chestnuts, cherry-cheeked apples, juicy oranges, luscious pears, immense twelfth-cakes, and seething bowls of punch, that made the chamber dim with their delicious steam. In easy state upon this couch, there sat a jolly Giant, glorious to see.

This friendly phantom then invites Scrooge to touch his robe, and instantaneously Ebenezer finds himself magically flying over London and beyond, holding onto the spirit's arm, where they witness how different people and families celebrate their Christmas Day. What follows in the next few pages is amongst the greatest episodes ever written by an English author. This is because *A Christmas Carol* was the first Christmas story in the world to feature a character flying wondrously over the city of London (something for which it is rarely given credit). Long before Raymond Briggs had written his delightful tale of *The Snowman,* Dickens had already written the ultimate flying sequence as Scrooge and The Ghost of Christmas Present fly through heavy snow over the spires and rooftops of the great city, and out beyond the English countryside, over moor, rock, and cliff.

"Scrooge's Flight"

Oil on canvas, 2006.

Copyright © artist Jonathan Barry.

This enchanted flight sequence is a book illustrator's dream, because as Scrooge and the spirit pass boldly over the edge of the cliff and out to sea – we are treated to a dizzying and dramatic spectacle as they circle a lighthouse below:

> To Scrooge's horror, looking back, he saw the last of the land, a frightful range of rocks, behind them; and his ears were deafened by the thundering of water, as it rolled and roared, and raged among the dreadful caverns it had worn, and fiercely tried to undermine the earth. Built upon a dismal reef of sunken rocks, some league or so from shore, on which the waters chafed and dashed, the wild year through, there stood a solitary lighthouse. Great heaps of sea-weed clung to its base, and storm-birds – born of the wind one might suppose, as sea-weed of the water – rose and fell about it, like the waves they skimmed.

Such a scene as this firmly demonstrates that had Dickens lived in the 20th century he could well have become a professional screenplay writer or even a movie director – so strong was his grasp of aerial and spatial dynamism.

His sense of visual drama is equally impressive. Take for example the cinematic quality of his writing when the story enters its final stages, and the third spirit appears before Scrooge (the Ghost of Christmas Yet to Come) to warn him of his impending doom. This silent phantom closely resembles the Grim Reaper of Death, and these intense Gothic episodes could almost pass as out-takes from a German horror movie by F.W. Murnau, or Fritz Lang in the 1920s (indeed it would have been fascinating to see what either of these eclectic movie directors would have done with *A Christmas Carol* had they filmed it).

I was profoundly disturbed as a teenager reading the scene where the robed phantom points his warning bony finger towards Scrooge's possible nightmarish end:

> The phantom pointed as before. He joined it once again, and wondering why and whither he had gone, accompanied it until they reached an iron gate. He paused to look around before entering. A churchyard. Here, then, the wretched man whose name he had now to learn, lay underneath the ground. It was a worthy place. Walled in by houses; overrun by grass and weeds, the growth of vegetation's death, not life; choked up with too much burying; fat with repleted appetite. A worthy place!

I will not assume that everyone on the globe knows how *A Christmas Carol* ends, and for anyone lucky enough to be reading it for the first time, I will leave that pleasure to be unwrapped. But if (like most of us) you are already well acquainted with its dénouement – you should still complete your whole experience by watching the marvellous movie from 1970 entitled 'Scrooge', starring the fabulous Albert Finney in the title role.

This adaptation has its flaws for sure (it is a musical production with several weak songs that add nothing to the storyline). But from an acting perspective and especially in the depiction of the ghost scenes – it is superb. The appearance of Alec Guinness as the ghost of Jacob Marley was inspired casting, with Guinness giving a powerful and bone chilling performance. Finney shines as Ebenezer, and Kenneth Moore delights as an effusive Ghost of Christmas Present. God bless us, Every One!

XII

Peter and Wendy
By
J.M. Barrie
(1860 – 1937)

A very ignorant man once said to me at a children's book launch one evening – "Why should I bother reading bloody *Peter Pan*, with that stupid looking pixie in green pants flying around a bedroom?" I pursed my lips, narrowed my eyes, and did my level best not to box him on the spot. To give myself great credit, I did manage to control that impulse, and I heard myself reply in a measured tone: - "Are you referring to the book or the play? There is a difference you know!" To which he looked at me contemptuously and walked off in a huff. Of course he did hit on one important point – the fact that *Peter and Wendy* has very much fallen off the reading lists of most children (and their parents) in the 21st century, something that is regrettable and sad.

Sir James Matthew Barrie was a Scotsman, a Calvinist, a graduate of Edinburgh University (where he received a Master's in Literature), an author, journalist, playwright, cricketer (of some note), passionate dog walker, voracious reader, noted London celebrity, baronet, and a member of the Order of Merit. Like all of the writers that I discuss in this book, he was hugely influential in his time. He had the ear of the Royal family, and every famous author of his generation.

Arthur Conan Doyle, H.G. Wells, Robert Louis Stevenson, and even Scott of the Antarctic were all personal friends of Barrie.

Before I delve into my favourite parts of the story, a few words need to be devoted to the origins and naming of this very famous yarn. There were four stages in its creative development. The character of 'Peter Pan' is first mentioned in Barrie's now forgotten adult novel *The Little White Bird*, published in 1902. He then took that character and expanded it into his famous play called *Peter Pan*, which hit the theatres in London in 1904. Following on from the huge success of the play (it earned over half a million pounds sterling in just two years) he turned it into a short children's book called *Peter Pan in Kensington Gardens*, which he released in 1906. But it was only in 1911 that he finally wrote a proper full-length book called *Peter and Wendy* (mistakenly referred to by everyone as *Peter Pan* ever since). It is that book, called *Peter and Wendy*, that we now read today as a timeless children's classic.

The naming of the famous boy who never wanted to grow up, came from a chance encounter that J.M. Barrie had in Kensington Gardens in London, when he was out walking his famous St. Bernard dog Porthos. It was a fine sunny afternoon in the summer of 1897, and Barrie (who was a very small man of just over five foot and three inches) frequently loved to roll around the park grass with Porthos (who was big enough to knock him down), when he was noticed frolicking with the dog by a nanny called Mary Hodgson, who happened to be walking her three charges through the park.

"Peter's Shadow"

Oil on canvas, 1999.

Copyright © artist Jonathan Barry.

She found Barrie's madcap antics quite amusing and got chatting to him. In so doing she introduced him to the three children in her care: George, Jack, and Peter Llewelyn Davies, who were the sons of Arthur and Sylvia Llewelyn Davies – a very respectable family who also lived close to Kensington Gardens. Barrie apparently delighted in pulling funny faces for the boys to make them laugh. This was the first of many meetings in Kensington Gardens between Mary Hodgson, the boys, and the well-known author. Barrie was soon introduced to their parents, and became good friends with the whole family. It was the beginning of a close lifelong relationship between Barrie and the Llewelyn Davies clan. In fact, when Arthur and Sylvia both died of cancer in 1907 and 1910 respectively, Barrie became the legal guardian of all the Llewelyn children (there were five boys in total).

Barrie invented the character of Peter Pan to specifically entertain George and John (Jack) Llewelyn Davies at their meetings in the park, and he told them (tongue-in-cheek) that their brother Peter could fly. It was therefore Peter Llewelyn Davies who inspired Barrie to invent the name 'Peter Pan'. This explains why Kensington Gardens features strongly in the book and why the park is forever connected to J.M. Barrie's legacy. In Chapter 3, of *Peter and Wendy*, Peter tells Wendy:

> 'I don't want ever to be a man,' he said with passion. I want always to be a little boy and to have fun. So I ran away to Kensington Gardens and lived a long long time among the fairies.[1]

By a happy coincidence, in 1993, when I came to prepare my own paintings and illustrations for *Peter and Wendy* I was already very familiar with Kensington Gardens and had been living in an apartment not far from Bayswater Road. J. M. Barrie lived at 100 Bayswater Road and I often passed this famous Victorian yellow brick house and the shining blue London County Council plaque commemorating his life there.

It is easy to see why Barrie was so inspired by Kensington Gardens, and on a summer's day it is a truly gorgeous place to take a sandwich, a flask of tea, and a sketch pad with pencils. I spent several days there visiting the same walks that Barrie frequented and did numerous pencil drawings, and some watercolours. I began my walks in Hyde Park, following the Serpentine River as far as the Serpentine Bridge, and concentrated my sketching mainly along the stretch of the river called The Long Water, which is a remarkable natural wildlife sanctuary, filled with the chatter of mallard ducks, pintail ducks, moorhens, geese, and mute swans. At certain points along the banks it is not uncommon to see the dipping and diving of swifts and swallows that have made the park their summer residence. If the sun became too strong beside the river, I sometimes made my way to a favourite shaded bench, where I would sit beside the celebrated statue of Peter Pan sculpted by Sir George Frampton in 1912. For some reason the hedge sparrows of Kensington Gardens love this spot, and would often join me in their dozens, hopping and chirping merrily on the paving at the base of the bronze sculpture.

"The Birds Have Flown"

Oil on canvas, 1999.

Copyright © artist Jonathan Barry.

One of my favourite views in Kensington Gardens is the cool shaded arbour of arched lime trees, better known as The Cradle Walk, (so called because it was a favourite walk of Edwardian nannies) which leads to the more formal gardens of Kensington Palace, including The Orangery designed by Queen Anne in 1704. I have no doubt that Mary Hodgson along with the Llewelyn boys, and accompanied by J.M. Barrie, must have walked this path on many occasions. Some days later, (and to complete the preparations for my artwork) I took a spin on the London Eye, and snapped many aerial photos of Big Ben, Westminster, and Tower Bridge to aid me in my oil paintings.

So what is it that makes *Peter and Wendy* rank as one of the most influential children's stories? To begin with, it was one of the first stories written by a British author to put centre stage *children* magically flying over the London skyline (I already highlighted in the previous chapter that Scrooge was the first *adult* character to fly magically over London). Why is this so significant? Because in the 20th and 21st centuries we rather arrogantly presume that children flying magically in any book or story has always been an established literary cliché. It was not always so – it mainly began (very imaginatively it should be added) with *Peter and Wendy*. Admittedly, the English children's writer Edith Nesbit, also wrote a popular story in 1904, called *The Phoenix and the Carpet,* in which a group of children have many adventures on a flying carpet. But its popularity faded, while the influence of *Peter and Wendy* grew. For the last one hundred years all children's authors that have written books with flying sequences (Travers' *Mary Poppins*, Ian Fleming's *Chitty Chitty Bang Bang*, Raymond Briggs' *The Snowman*, J.K Rowling's *The Chamber of Secrets*) – all were influenced by J.M. Barrie.

It still remains for me a nostalgic thrill to read the scene in Chapter 3, of *Peter and Wendy*, where Peter Pan and Tinkerbell, for the first time fly magically around the nursery looking for Peter's shadow. Barrie's play on light and darkness is most effective here:

> There was another light in the room now, a thousand times brighter than the night-lights, and in the time we have taken to say this, it has been in all the drawers in the nursery, looking for Peter's shadow...it made this light by flashing around so quickly, but when it came to rest for a second you saw it was a fairy, no longer than your hand, but still growing. It was a girl called Tinker Bell exquisitely gowned in a skeleton leaf...

You cannot imagine the joy and wonder that this scene brought to juvenile readers in 1911, who finally got in book form what many of them had always dreamt about - what must it be like to be able to fly? And here J.M. Barrie gave them that answer. Equally, this scene perfectly encapsulates the nostalgic comfort of Edwardian nurseries with their deliciously English nod towards everything that brought confidence and security to the British Empire's children: wooden redcoat soldiers (which gave assurance of their imperial dominance in the colonies), sturdy rocking horses (for future cavalry riders in India), tin drums (for the future

"Marooner's Rock"

Oil on canvas, 2000.

Copyright © artist Jonathan Barry.

infantry man), and toy White Star Liners (showing the industrial confidence of Edwardian Britain pre Titanic). Every English child wanted to be in that room and part of that experience.

While Barrie became a pillar of the establishment later in life, it is fascinating that in *Peter and Wendy* he was very keen to flirt with (even promote) the theme of freedom – including freedom of thought and actions. For example, having woken up Wendy with their flying antics in the nursery, we get a nice taste of her personality in the following pages. Wendy is no shrinking violet and she clearly knows how to deal with Peter's cheekiness (which sometimes borders on arrogance), and she becomes a maternal figure taking charge of the Lost Boys in Neverland, and putting Captain James Hook firmly in his place. Indeed Wendy displays many of the characteristics of the suffragettes and feminists who were gaining ground and influence in London circles after 1911. This is one of the reasons why Wendy remained a very popular fictional character amongst teenage girl readers of the Edwardian era, some of whom would go on to become suffragettes.

Having introduced Peter and Tinker Bell into the narrative, Barrie then sets the scene for the flight over London, in Chapter 4, called 'The Flight'. Outside it is a crisp bright winters night, and with a sprinkling of fairy dust Peter encourages Wendy, John and Michael to follow his lead and leave their beds. Pushing the windows wide open Peter shouts:

'Come', he cried imperiously, and soared out at once into

the night, followed by John and Michael and Wendy. Mr. and Mrs. Darling and Nana rushed into the nursery too late…

'Second to the right, and straight on till morning.'

At first his companions trusted him implicitly, and so great were the delights of flying that they wasted time circling around church spires or any other tall objects on the way that took their fancy.

As they clear the myriad lights of Westminster Bridge, the cool blue tiles of Big Ben, and the dramatic Gothic spires of Westminster Abbey, Peter audaciously takes them on what becomes an awfully big adventure across the London skyline and out eventually onto the sea. It is lovely how Peter teases and guides the children across the waves, showing them how to sleep on the wind while flying on their backs, or mischievously snatching bits of food out of bird's mouths to give them in case they get hungry. Certainly, these pagan Pan-like qualities that Peter displays while flying are enough to make Wendy slightly wary of him. Indeed, what makes Peter Pan an interesting children's character is his slightly dangerous God-like powers and unpredictable nature. He is one part elf, one part wizard, one part pixie, and one part human. Their flight reaches a peak where they swirl with consummate joy in and out of the rose tinted clouds as they approach Neverland.

Another strength in the story is Barrie's very fine descriptions of idealised natural landscapes. Whether it is seas, islands, rocks, sunsets, or lagoons – he is as capable as Robert Louis Stevenson in bringing them to life. As they descend from the clouds and start their approach to Neverland we get a warm feeling for the place:

> Wendy and John and Michael stood on tiptoe in the air to get their first sight of the island. Strange to say, they all recognised it at once, and until fear fell upon them they hailed it, not as something long dreamt of and seen at last, but as a familiar friend to whom they were returning home for the holidays.

No sooner do they land on the island than we get a marvellous description of one of the funniest, most dastardly, and vainglorious villains in children's literature – the incomparable Captain James Hook. Matching him up against the plucky brave charisma of Peter was a master stroke on Barrie's behalf. Considering he is only a scoundrel of a children's tale Barrie goes to some length to give us a beautifully detailed description in Chapter 5, not only of Hook's physical appearance, but his personality disorders too:

> In person he was cadaverous and blackavised, and his hair was dressed in long curls, which at a little distance looked like black candles, and gave a singularly threatening expression to his handsome countenance. His eyes were of the blue of forget-me-knot, and of a profound melancholy, save when he was plunging his hook into you, at which time two red spots appeared in them and lit them up horribly.

Hook is a wonderfully neurotic blackguard - long before the psychological analysis of literary villains became commonplace in the bestsellers of the 20th century. Indeed, his narcissism, cruelty, childishness, insecurity, and pathological tendencies remind me uncannily of a certain 21st century US President with badly dyed blond hair, and a burnt orange face (who we need not name). The scenes where Hook chides and upbraids his fellow pirates on The Jolly Roger are very funny. And like all thugs and bullies – when he is confronted by integrity and the courage of an honest heart - he quickly collapses into a cowardly heap of frayed nerves, as demonstrated in the stand-off between Peter and Hook when they fight together on top of Marooner's Rock:

> ...Strangely, it was not in the water that they met. Hook rose to the rock to breathe, and at the same moment Peter scaled it on the opposite side...But Peter had no sinking, he had one feeling only, gladness; and he gnashed his pretty teeth with joy. Quick as thought he snatched a knife from Hooke's belt and was about to drive it home...

What happens next? You will just have to read the story to find out.

Rather than mention any of the many movies or animated cartoons that the book inspired – I would instead highly recommend a superb docudrama TV miniseries made by the BBC in 1978, called 'The Lost Boys' which deals most sensitively with J.M. Barrie's relationship with the Llewelyn Davies family. It rightly received rave reviews at the time. Ian Holm gives a career defining performance as J.M. Barrie (for which he won a best performance award in 1979 with the Royal Television Society).

Thank you for considering my thoughts on these much loved stories, and I hope that you now feel inspired enough to wander freely through these literary fields of imaginative gold. Pop on the kettle, kick off your shoes, and enter a world of splendid joy. You will not regret it.

REFERENCES*

CHAPTER I
1. Emily Brontë, *Wuthering Heights*, London, 1879. Published by Smith, Elder & Co.

CHAPTER II
1. Kenneth Grahame, *The Wind In The Willows*, London, 1923. Published by Methuen & Co. Ltd.

CHAPTER III
1. H.G. Wells, *The War Of The Worlds*, London, 1898. Published by William Heinemann. 1st Edition.

CHAPTER IV
1. Arthur Conan Doyle, *The Hound Of The Baskervilles*, London, 1902. Published by George Newnes Ltd. 1st Edition.

CHAPTER V
1. Oscar Wilde, *The Happy Prince And Other Stories*, London, 1913. Published by Duckworth & Co.

CHAPTER VI
1. M.R.James, *Oh, Whistle, And I'll Come To You, My Lad*, from *Ghost Stories Of An Antiquary*, London, 1905. Published by Edward Arnold. 1st Edition.

CHAPTER VII
1. Charles Dickens, *Great Expectations*, London, 1907. Published by Chapman & Hall Ltd.

CHAPTER VIII
1. Bram Stoker, *Dracula*, London, 1912.
    Published by William Rider & Son Ltd. 9th Edition.

CHAPTER IX
1. Robert Louis Stevenson, *The Strange Case Of Dr. Jekyll And Mr. Hyde*, from *Dr. Jekyll And Mr. Hyde With Other Fables*, London, 1897. Published by Longmans, Green, & Co.

CHAPTER X
1. Lewis Carroll, *Alice's Adventures In Wonderland*, London, 1907. Published by Macmillan & Co Ltd.

CHAPTER XI
1. Charles Dickens, *A Christmas Carol In Prose, Being A Ghost Story Of Christmas*, Leipzig, 1846. Published by Bernard Tauchnitz. The Copyright Edition.

CHAPTER XII
1. J. M. Barrie, *Peter and Wendy*, London, 1911. Published by Hodder & Stoughton. 1st Edition.

*All quotations in each chapter are taken from the specific edition identified above. These form part of the private collection of books owned by the author.

ABOUT THE AUTHOR

Jonathan Barry is the acclaimed author of the horror novel *'The Devil's Hoof – A Gothic Tale'*, and he is an internationally renowned professional artist and book illustrator. He specializes in illustrating famous classic novels and literature, and has illustrated over seventy books in his career. These include such famous titles as: *Wuthering Heights, Dracula, Frankenstein, Peter Pan, The Wind in the Willows, The Hound of the Baskervilles, The Adventures of Sherlock Holmes, The Return of Sherlock Holmes, Alice's Adventure in Wonderland, Cinderella, Sleeping Beauty, Beauty and the Beast,* and many more.

Jonathan is the only living Irish book illustrator to have sold his original artwork at *Sotheby's* famous auction house on New Bond Street in London, where he has sold nine of his oil paintings to date. His paintings have appeared in over one hundred and fifty international newspapers and magazines, including *The Wall Street Journal* and *The London Times*. On television his illustrations have appeared in the British soaps *EastEnders* and *Coronation Street*. He is a passionate exponent of the Gothic horror genre, and since 1999, has been running a Gothic Literary Book Club in Dublin, where he lives. If you would like to purchase a print of the paintings in this book, email the artist below.

Jonathan welcomes feedback. Email him at:
jonathanbarrypainter@gmail.com

Acclaimed novel by Jonathan Barry

The Devil's Hoof
A Gothic Tale

In the bleak winter of 1741, in the isolated village of Glenboyne, a series of horrific murders occur in the Dublin mountains. Daniel Parsons, an English official, is dispatched from Dublin Castle to investigate the crimes, and finds a community in the grip of terror, and unwilling to talk. What should he make of the rumours of a demonic creature sworn by the locals to be seen and heard at the scene of each killing? And why do bonfires light up the midnight sky at the summit of the mountaintop? But the truth is darker than he could ever have imagined.

"... cinematic in quality..."
Sunday Independent